Cybersecurity
100 Interview Questions

X.Y. Wang

Contents

6 Guru   147

Chapter 1

Introduction

In today's rapidly evolving digital landscape, cybersecurity has become a crucial component of modern society. The increasing dependence on technology and the internet has resulted in a growing need for professionals who can effectively safeguard our digital world. As a result, cybersecurity professionals are in high demand, and the need for individuals who can think critically and navigate the complexities of this field has never been greater.

In this book, "Cybersecurity: 100 Interview Questions", we have compiled a comprehensive collection of questions that cover various aspects of cybersecurity. Designed to equip both aspiring and experienced cybersecurity professionals with the knowledge and skills needed to excel in their careers, this book delves into topics ranging from basic cybersecurity concepts to advanced techniques and strategies.

The book is divided into five sections based on the level of expertise:

Basic: This section covers fundamental concepts and terms in cybersecurity, providing a solid foundation for

- understanding the field.

- Intermediate: Building on the basics, this section delves into more complex topics and concepts, exploring various cybersecurity practices and methodologies.

- Advanced: Here, we examine more sophisticated topics in cybersecurity, such as digital forensics, threat hunting, and securing emerging technologies.

- Expert: This section provides insights into high-level cybersecurity strategies and approaches, as well as the challenges associated with managing security in large-scale, complex environments.

- Guru: In the final section, we delve into cutting-edge topics and emerging trends in cybersecurity, addressing the future of the field and its potential ethical considerations.

Each question is designed to challenge your understanding of cybersecurity and help you prepare for interviews, certifications, or simply to deepen your knowledge. Through these 100 questions, you will gain a comprehensive understanding of the cybersecurity landscape and be better equipped to address the challenges that lie ahead.

As you explore this book, keep in mind that the field of cybersecurity is constantly evolving, and staying current on the latest trends and developments is essential. We hope that "Cybersecurity: 100 Interview Questions" serves as a valuable resource in your journey as a cybersecurity professional, and we wish you success in your career endeavors.

Chapter 2

Basic

2.1 What is cybersecurity and why is it important?

Cybersecurity is the practice of protecting computers, servers, mobile devices, electronic systems, networks and data from digital attacks, theft or damage. Cybersecurity includes a range of defensive tactics, technologies and practices that are designed to safeguard computer systems, networks and data from unauthorized access, use, disclosure, disruption, modification or destruction.

In today's digital age, cybersecurity is vitally important for both individuals and organizations. As more and more information and services are moved online, the risks associated with cybersecurity breaches continue to grow. A cyber attack can result in significant negative consequences, including financial loss, intellectual property theft, reputational damage, business disruption, legal liability or even harm to individuals.

In recent years, we have seen an increase in the number and severity of cyber attacks. These attacks can come from a variety of sources, including criminal hackers, state-sponsored actors, and insiders. Some common tactics used in cyber attacks include malware, phishing, social engineering, denial of service attacks, and ransomware.

Examples of high-profile data breaches in recent years include the Marriott data breach which resulted in theft of personal data from up to 500 million customers, the Equifax breach which exposed the sensitive data of 147 million Americans, and the Yahoo breach which compromised the security of all 3 billion users accounts.

Cybersecurity is essential not only for protecting digital assets but also for ensuring the overall security and privacy of individuals and organizations. It is critical that everyone takes steps to protect themselves from cyber threats through practicing good cybersecurity hygiene, updating software regularly, using strong passwords and two-factor authentication, avoiding public Wi-Fi, and being cautious of unexpected emails or messages. Additionally, businesses should invest in cybersecurity tools and training for their employees, conduct regular cybersecurity risk assessments, and make sure to follow industry best practices and standards.

2.2   What are the main types of cybersecurity threats?

There are numerous types of cybersecurity threats that organizations need to be aware of in order to protect their digital assets. Here are some of the main types of cybersecurity threats:

1. Malware: Malware is short for "malicious software" and includes viruses, trojans, worms, and other types of malicious code that are designed to cause harm to your computer system, steal information, or extort money from you.

2. Phishing: Phishing is when cybercriminals try to trick you into giving them your sensitive information by sending you a message that looks like it's from a trusted source, such as a bank or email provider. The message may contain a link that takes you to a fake website where you're asked to enter your login credentials or other personal information.

3. Denial-of-service (DoS) and Distributed Denial-of-service (DDoS) attacks: These types of attacks are designed to overwhelm a network or system with traffic and prevent legitimate users from accessing it. DoS attacks come from a single source, while DDoS attacks come from multiple sources, making them harder to defend against.

4. Man-in-the-middle (MitM) attacks: These attacks involve intercepting communications between two parties and stealing sensitive information, such as login credentials or financial information. MitM attacks can occur on both public and private networks and can be difficult to detect.

5. SQL injection: A SQL injection is a type of attack where

a cybercriminal injects malicious code into a website's SQL database, in order to steal or manipulate sensitive data. SQL injection attacks are often successful because many websites don't sanitize user input properly.

6. Zero-day attacks: These are attacks that exploit a vulnerability that is unknown to the software vendor or cybersecurity community. Zero-day attacks are often the most dangerous type of cyber threat, as no patch or fix yet exists to mitigate the vulnerability.

7. Ransomware: Ransomware is a type of malware that infects a computer system and encrypts the victim's files, making them unreadable. The attacker then demands a ransom payment, usually in cryptocurrency, in exchange for the decryption key.

These are just some of the many types of cybersecurity threats that organizations need to be aware of and prepared to defend against. By implementing best practices and staying up-to-date on the latest threats and attack methods, organizations can better protect their digital assets and minimize the risk of a successful cyber attack.

2.3   What is the CIA triad in cybersecurity?

The CIA triad is a foundational concept in cybersecurity that stands for Confidentiality, Integrity, and Availability. It is used to evaluate and assess the security posture of an organization's systems, data, and networks.

1. Confidentiality: Confidentiality ensures that sensitive infor-

mation is protected from unauthorized access, disclosure, and theft. It is essential to maintain secrecy and privacy of information such as personal data, financial information, and company trade secrets. In cybersecurity, confidentiality is achieved by deploying access control methods such as authentication, authorization, and encryption. For example, in online banking, a user's account information is kept confidential by implementing two-factor authentication and encryption for all transactions.

2. Integrity: Integrity ensures the accuracy and consistency of data and information over time. It is concerned with ensuring that data are accurate, and has not been altered, modified or corrupted. In cybersecurity, integrity is maintained through mechanisms such as data backups, change management policies, and data validation procedures. For example, cryptographic hashes are used to ensure the integrity of data in transit or at rest.

3. Availability: Availability ensures that data and systems are available and accessible to authorized users when they need them. It means that the systems are up and running, and that access to data and system resources is provided within the defined authorization and security parameters. Availability is essential in critical systems such as healthcare and finance. In cybersecurity, availability is achieved by implementing load-balancing mechanisms, redundancy, and failover systems. For example, Distributed Denial of Service (DDoS) attacks often target the availability of a system by overwhelming it with traffic. Organizations deploy technologies such as Intrusion Prevention Systems (IPS) and firewalls to protect against such attacks.

In conclusion, the CIA triad is a critical concept in cybersecurity that helps to ensure the confidentiality, integrity, and availability of data, systems, and networks. Implementing CIA triad principles safeguards against unauthorized access, data breaches, and other cybersecurity risks.

2.4   Can you explain the difference between vulnerability, threat, and risk?

Vulnerability, threat, and risk are three important concepts in cybersecurity. While they are often used interchangeably, they actually have different meanings.

Vulnerability refers to a weakness in a system or application that can be exploited by an attacker. Vulnerabilities can exist in software, hardware, or even human behavior. For example, a software vulnerability could be a flaw in the code that allows an attacker to gain unauthorized access to sensitive data. A hardware vulnerability might be a flaw in a processor that allows an attacker to bypass security measures. A human vulnerability could be an employee who fails to follow proper security protocols.

Threat refers to the likelihood that a vulnerability will be exploited. A threat actor is a malicious individual or group who takes advantage of a vulnerability in order to compromise a system. Threats can come from all sorts of sources, including cybercriminals, nation-states, and even disgruntled employees. Examples of threats include ransomware attacks, phishing scams, and DDoS (distributed denial of service) attacks.

Risk, meanwhile, refers to the potential for harm or damage that could result from a successful attack. This harm can be financial, reputational, or even physical. Risk is calculated by assessing the likelihood of a threat occurring and the impact that it would have. For example, a company that stores sensitive customer data might have a high risk of a data breach occurring, since the consequences of such a breach could be severe.

To summarize:

- Vulnerability is a weakness in a system.

- Threat is the likelihood of that weakness being exploited.

- Risk is the potential harm or damage that could result from a successful attack.

It's important for organizations to understand these concepts because they can help them identify and prioritize potential security risks. By identifying vulnerabilities and assessing the likelihood and potential impact of threats, organizations can take steps to mitigate their security risks and protect their assets.

2.5   What are some common types of malware and their functions?

Malware, short for "malicious software," is any software that is specifically designed to harm or disrupt computer systems. Here are some common types of malware along with their functions:

1. Viruses - Viruses are one of the oldest and most well-known types of malware. They spread by infecting other files or programs and can cause a variety of problems, such as deleting

files, stealing personal information, or causing the computer to crash.

2. Worms - Worms are similar to viruses, but they have the ability to spread on their own without infecting other files or programs. They often spread through email attachments, instant messaging, or social media, and can cause damage to a computer or network by replicating themselves and using up resources.

3. Trojans - Trojans are disguised as legitimate programs or files, but they contain malicious code that can be used to steal sensitive information, install other malware, or even take control of the computer remotely. Examples of trojans include fake antivirus software, keyloggers, and remote access trojans (RATs).

4. Ransomware - Ransomware is a type of malware that locks the victim's files or threatens to publish them unless a ransom is paid. It often arrives as an email attachment or through a compromised website, and can be devastating for individuals or businesses.

5. Adware - Adware is a type of malware that displays unwanted or intrusive ads on a computer or mobile device. It can slow down the device, track user activities, and expose the user to other types of malware.

6. Spyware - Spyware is a type of malware that is designed to secretly collect information about the victim's computer or mobile device, often for the purpose of stealing sensitive data such as passwords, bank account details, or personal information.

It's important to note that malware is constantly evolving, and new variants or strains of existing malware are constantly being created. It's essential to use antivirus software, update software regularly, and practice safe browsing habits to protect against malware attacks.

2.6   What is the difference between a virus, worm, and Trojan?

All three are types of malicious software (malware), but they differ in their behavior and method of propagation.

A virus is a type of malware that spreads by infecting files or systems. When an infected file is opened or executed, the virus code is activated and can replicate itself by infecting other files on the same system or network. Viruses can also have a payload that can cause damage, such as deleting files, stealing data, or crashing the system. For example, the famous "ILOVEYOU" virus in 2000 infected millions of computers worldwide and caused billions of dollars in damage by overwriting and deleting files.

A worm, on the other hand, spreads by taking advantage of security vulnerabilities in networked systems. Once it infects one computer, it can automatically propagate itself to other vulnerable systems on the same network, without the need for human interaction. Worms can also have a payload that can cause damage, such as creating backdoors for remote access, stealing sensitive information, or launching DDoS attacks. For example, the Wannacry ransomware worm in 2017 exploited a vulnerability in Microsoft Windows to infect over 200,000 computers in a matter of days and encrypt their files, demanding payment in exchange for the decryption key.

A Trojan (or Trojan horse) is a type of malware that disguises itself as legitimate software, such as a game or utility program, to trick users into downloading and installing it. Once installed, the Trojan can perform a variety of malicious actions, such as stealing passwords, logging keystrokes, taking screenshots, or opening backdoors for remote access. Trojans do not typically replicate themselves like viruses or worms, but they can be used to deliver other types of malware or to create botnets for further attacks. For example, the Zeus Trojan in 2007 was capable of stealing banking credentials and other sensitive information, and was responsible for millions of dollars in fraud.

In summary, viruses, worms, and Trojans are all forms of malware, but they have different propagation methods and behaviors. Knowing the differences can help in identifying and mitigating their risks.

2.7   What is a firewall, and how does it help protect a network?

A firewall is a network security system that monitors and controls incoming and outgoing network traffic based on predetermined security rules. It acts as a barrier between an organization's internal network and the public internet, allowing only authorized traffic to pass through while blocking or filtering out unwanted traffic such as viruses, malware, or hackers attempting to breach the network.

There are several types of firewalls, such as packet-filtering firewalls, stateful firewalls, application-level firewalls, and next-generation firewalls (NGFW). Packet-filtering firewalls are the most basic type and they determine whether to allow or deny traffic based on pre-determined criteria, such as the source and destination IP addresses and ports. Stateful firewalls are more advanced, as they keep track of the state of network connections and allow only authorized connections. Application-level firewalls are designed to examine the content of the incoming and outgoing traffic to determine whether it is safe or not, whereas NGFWs use a combination of several technologies to detect and block more sophisticated attacks.

Firewalls help protect a network by providing a secure perimeter defense. By preventing unauthorized access to a network, it minimizes the risk of cyber attacks, data breaches, and malware infections. For instance, if a firewall is configured to block incoming traffic from a suspicious IP address, it can prevent a hacker from getting access to sensitive data stored on the company's servers. Firewalls are also useful in preventing denial-of-service (DoS) attacks, where the attacker floods the network with traffic to cause it to crash. By filtering out unwanted traffic, firewalls can keep the network running smoothly.

Overall, firewalls play a crucial role in cybersecurity as they help protect a company's networks, data, and resources from unauthorized access or attacks from malicious actors. It is important to maintain and update firewalls regularly to ensure they provide maximum protection and are able to keep up with the evolving threat landscape.

2.8   What is the purpose of encryption, and how does it work?

Encryption is the process of transforming information into a code that can only be decoded and interpreted by authorized parties. The purpose of encryption is to ensure confidentiality and integrity of information, especially when it is being transmitted over a network or stored in an insecure environment.

Encryption works by using an algorithm to scramble the original text or data, known as plaintext, into an encoded message or ciphertext. This ciphertext can only be read by someone who possesses the key or password that can decode the message back into the original plaintext.

There are two main types of encryption: symmetric key encryption and asymmetric key encryption. Symmetric key encryption uses the same key to encrypt and decrypt the message, while asymmetric key encryption uses two different keys, one for encryption and one for decryption.

Let's take an example of symmetric key encryption. Imagine that you want to send a confidential message to a friend using a messaging app. You both agree on a secret key to use for encryption and decryption. When you type your message, the app uses the key to encrypt the message and sends it over the network. When your friend receives the message, they use the same key to decrypt the message and read the original plaintext.

Asymmetric key encryption, also known as public key cryptography, is a more secure method of encryption. In this method, there are two keys: a public key and a private key. The public key is available to anyone, while the private key is kept secret.

To send an encrypted message, the sender uses the recipient's public key to encrypt the message. The recipient then uses their private key to decrypt the message.

In conclusion, encryption is a vital tool for cybersecurity to keep sensitive information safe and secure. Encryption provides confidentiality, integrity, and authenticity of data, ensuring that only authorized parties can access and interpret the information.

2.9   What is the difference between symmetric and asymmetric encryption?

Symmetric and asymmetric encryption are two different methods of encrypting and decrypting data.

Symmetric encryption uses a single secret key known to both the sender and the recipient. The same key is used for both encrypting and decrypting the data. In other words, the key is symmetrical in the sense that it is the same on both ends. The advantage of symmetric encryption is that it is faster and simpler than asymmetric encryption, making it suitable for encrypting large amounts of data. However, the biggest disadvantage is that if the key falls into the wrong hands, the data can be easily decrypted.

Asymmetric encryption, on the other hand, uses two different keys a public key and a private key to encrypt and decrypt data. The public key is shared and used by anyone who wants to send a message to the receiver, while the private key is kept secret and used only by the receiver to decrypt the data. The public key is used to encrypt the data, while the private key is used to decrypt it. The advantage of asymmetric encryption is that it is more secure than symmetric encryption, as the private key is kept secret and can only be used by the intended recipient. The disadvantage is that it is slower and more complex than symmetric encryption.

In summary, the main difference between symmetric and asymmetric encryption is the number of keys used. Symmetric encryption uses a single key, while asymmetric encryption uses two keys. Symmetric encryption is faster and simpler, but less secure than asymmetric encryption, which is slower and more complex, but more secure.

For example, in symmetric encryption, the sender and recipient might agree to use a key such as "SECRET" to encrypt and decrypt their messages. In asymmetric encryption, the sender would use the recipient's public key to encrypt the message, which only the recipient can decrypt using their private key.

2.10   What are some common types of phishing attacks and how can you identify them?

Phishing is a type of social engineering attack where an attacker aims to trick the victim into revealing their personal or confidential information such as username, password, credit card details, or other sensitive information. Here are some of the most common types of phishing attacks:

1. Email phishing: This is the most common type of phishing attack where an attacker sends an email that looks like a legit-

To give an example, suppose a user needs to connect to a public Wi-Fi network, but they do not trust the security of the network. They can use a VPN to create a secure tunnel and encrypt their internet traffic, preventing unauthorized access to their online data. Another example could be when an employee works remotely and needs to access company resources securely, they can use a VPN to create a secure connection to the company's internal network.

Overall, a VPN is an essential tool for anyone who values their online privacy and security.

2.12 What is the principle of least privilege, and why is it important in cybersecurity?

The principle of least privilege is a cybersecurity principle that states that people, systems, and applications should be granted the minimum amount of access and permissions required to perform their job functions or tasks. This means that users and systems should only be able to access the data and resources that are necessary for their work and nothing more.

The idea behind the principle of least privilege is to reduce the attack surface and limit the damage that can result from a security breach. By granting the minimum level of access required, an organization can limit the potential damage that can be caused by a cyber attack. For example, if a user only has access to certain data and resources, an attacker who gains access to that user's account will only be able to access that limited set of data and resources, limiting the potential damage.

Additionally, the principle of least privilege helps to ensure that users can only make changes that are necessary for their tasks, reducing the likelihood of accidental or intentional damage to systems or data. It also helps enforce the principle of separation of duties, which requires that no one person can perform all aspects of a critical business process, and reduces the likelihood of fraud or other insider threats.

In practical terms, the principle of least privilege involves assigning user permissions based on their job roles and responsibilities, and regularly reviewing and removing unnecessary permissions. It also involves using tools and technologies like firewalls, access control lists, and role-based access control (RBAC) to manage and enforce user access and permissions.

Overall, the principle of least privilege is an important cybersecurity practice that can help organizations limit the damage of cyberattacks and reduce the risk of insider threats.

2.13   What is social engineering, and how can it be mitigated?

Social engineering refers to the use of psychological manipulation or deception to trick individuals into divulging confidential information or performing an action that benefits an attacker. Attackers will often employ social engineering tactics to gain sensitive data (such as login credentials, passwords or credit card numbers), install malware, or gain access to secure systems or facilities. Cybercriminals may use several social engineering techniques, such as phishing attacks, pretexting, baiting, and scareware, among others.

Phishing attacks involve the use of fake emails or websites that appear legitimate, aimed at tricking users into providing personal and sensitive information, such as bank account passwords. The attacker may use a pretext to trick the user into divulging their personal data, such as posing as a bank representative, government official, or company employee.

Pretexting involves the creation of a fabricated scenario or pretext to gain the targets trust, for example, creating a fake scenario and presenting the potential victim as a beneficiary of a non-existent reward, forcing them to provide personal information.

Baiting involves luring the victim with an attractive lure, such as an offer of free software, free subscriptions or other merchandise, with the goal of stealing their credentials or infecting their system with malware.

Scareware involves falsifying software or security alerts that cause users to panic and take immediate action, often resulting in them exposing their information or downloading malicious software.

To mitigate social engineering attacks, companies and individuals can take several measures, including:

1. Create awareness: educate employees or individuals about the various social engineering tactics and the associated risks of cyber attacks. Training can include phishing simulations or ethical hacking to educate employees about how hackers operate.

2. Use Multi-Factor Authentication (MFA): rather than relying solely on passwords, MFA requires a subject to provide multiple

pieces of authentication before logging in (like a fingerprint, one time password).

3. Implement security protocols and strategies: a combination of firewalls and endpoint protection, regular software updates, and access controls would go a long way in protecting an organization from social engineering attacks.

4. Enhance checking and countersigning: checks and countersignatures need to be in place to ensure that all requests requiring authorization are properly vetted and verified.

5. Engage suppliers: companies should have a robust security program in place that includes security best practices by their vendors and suppliers.

6. Create and implement security policies: companies need to create social engineering guidelines that spell out sanctioned security measures, practices, and protocols related to the handling of sensitive data.

In summary, social engineering attacks often rely on human emotions and weaknesses; therefore, enhancing awareness, regular training, and implementing security protocols and best practices can reduce the likelihood of such attacks.

2.14   What is multi-factor authentication (MFA), and why is it important?

Multi-factor authentication (MFA) is a security process that requires multiple forms of authentication in order to gain access to a particular system or application. These forms of authentication can include something the user knows, such as a password or PIN, something they have, such as a security token or smart card, or something they are, such as biometric data like fingerprint, retina or facial recognition.

The purpose of MFA is to add an additional layer of security in order to prevent unauthorized access to sensitive data or systems. This way, even if someone has obtained a users username and password, they cannot gain access without the additional form of authentication.

MFA is important because most security breaches occur due to weak, stolen or compromised passwords. Passwords can be easily guessed, phished or stolen with the help of a hackers sophisticated techniques. In contrast, MFA provides an added layer of security, safeguarding against cyber-attacks that may occur due to a user's weak password or a data breach exposing passwords. Multi-factor authentication makes the users data more secure, and it is an essential requirement for regulatory compliance in many industries.

For example, a bank may employ multi-factor authentication for its online banking services to help ensure customer account data is only accessed by authorized persons. With MFA, a typical login process would involve the user typing in their username and password as usual, but they would also have to enter an additional one-time password or verify their identity through their phone or other authentication method.

Overall, MFA is a crucial security control that organizations should include as an important part of their security strategies to provide an additional layer of security to protect their sensitive data, networks, and systems.

2.15 What are some best practices for creating strong passwords?

Creating strong passwords is an essential security practice that can help protect your online accounts and sensitive information from cyber attacks. Here are some best practices for creating strong passwords:

1. Length: Use a minimum of 12 characters. The longer the password, the harder it is for hackers to guess or crack it.

2. Complexity: Use a mix of uppercase and lowercase letters, numbers, and special characters such as @, #, $, &, *, etc. Avoid using common words and phrases, names, dates, or information that can be easily associated with you, such as your birthdate or address.

3. Don't reuse passwords: Use unique passwords for each online account. This minimizes the risk of attackers gaining access to multiple accounts if one password is compromised.

4. Use a password manager: A password manager can help generate and securely store strong passwords so you don't have to remember them all.

5. Two-factor authentication: Use two-factor authentication wherever possible. This adds an extra layer of security by requiring users to enter a code generated through a separate authentication device or service.

6. Use passphrases: A passphrase is a long sequence of words or a sentence. They are easier to remember and harder to crack than traditional passwords. For example, "My first car was a

Toyota Corolla from 2005" is a strong passphrase.

7. Don't share your passwords: It's important to keep your passwords private and not share them with anyone, even friends or family members.

Overall, creating strong passwords is a critical component of online security. By following these best practices, you can help prevent unauthorized access to your accounts and protect your personal information from cyber threats.

2.16 What are some common methods of protecting a system or network from unauthorized access?

There are several methods that can be used to protect a system or network from unauthorized access:

1. Passwords: Passwords are the most common and basic form of access control. They are used to ensure that only authorized users can access a system or network. Passwords should be strong and complex, and users should be required to change them regularly.

2. Multifactor authentication: Multifactor authentication involves using two or more forms of authentication to verify a users identity. For example, a user may be required to enter a password and then provide a fingerprint or other biometric scan.

3. Firewalls: Firewalls are hardware or software devices that control access to a network by examining incoming and outgo-

ing traffic. They can be configured to block traffic from unauthorized sources or to allow traffic only to specific ports and protocols.

4. Intrusion detection systems: Intrusion detection systems (IDS) are used to detect unauthorized access attempts or other suspicious activity on a network. They can be configured to send alerts to administrators when such activity is detected.

5. Encryption: Encryption is the process of encoding data to prevent unauthorized access. This can be used to protect sensitive data that is being transmitted over a network or stored on a device.

6. Access control lists: Access control lists (ACL) are used to control access to specific resources on a network. For example, an ACL may be used to restrict access to a particular folder or file to only certain users or groups.

7. Patch management: Patch management refers to the process of applying software updates and patches to systems and applications to fix known vulnerabilities. This can help prevent unauthorized access to a system or network through known vulnerabilities.

Examples:

- A financial institution may use multifactor authentication to ensure that only authorized users can access their banking system. In addition to a password, users may be required to provide a fingerprint scan or a one-time password generated by a mobile app.

- A company may use firewalls to control access to their internal network. They may configure the firewall to block traffic from known malicious IP addresses and to allow traffic only to certain ports and protocols.

- An organization may use an IDS to detect unauthorized access attempts or other suspicious activity on their network. When the IDS detects such activity, it may send alerts to administrators who can investigate and take action to prevent further unauthorized access.

- A healthcare provider may use encryption to protect patient data that is being transmitted over a network. This ensures that even if the data is intercepted by an unauthorized user, it cannot be read without the proper decryption key.

- A university may use access control lists to restrict access to certain resources on their network. For example, they may restrict access to a particular research database to only certain faculty members or researchers who have been granted access.

2.17 Can you describe the difference between an intrusion detection system (IDS) and an intrusion prevention system (IPS)?

An Intrusion Detection System (IDS) is a security technology that can detect potentially malicious activities or violations of policy in a network or system. An IDS generally works by examining network activity and comparing it against signature-based rules or behavioral anomalies. When an IDS detects an event that matches a defined pattern or behavior, it issues an alert or notification to security personnel or administrators so they can take action to investigate and mitigate the potential threat.

Some examples of IDS technologies include:

- - Signature-based IDS

- - Anomaly-based IDS

- - Host-based IDS

- - Network-based IDS

On the other hand, an Intrusion Prevention System (IPS) is a technology that actively blocks or prevents unauthorized access or malicious activity on a network or system. IPS is an extension of IDS, meaning it has the same detection capabilities but goes a step further by preventing malicious activity. IPS can achieve this through various means such as blocking access to known malicious IP addresses, blocking suspicious traffic based on predefined rules, or modifying access policies in real-time.

Examples of IPS technologies include:

- - Network-based IPS

- - Host-based IPS

The main difference between IDS and IPS is that IDS solely focuses on detecting potential threats, whereas IPS not only detects threats but also prevents them from happening. In other words, an IPS is more effective because it takes immediate action to stop an attack, whereas an IDS relies on a human operator to take action after observing a threat.

It's worth noting that both IDS and IPS can work together to provide better security outcomes. By delivering real-time alerts and enabling automatic responses such as blocking an IP address or quarantining a device, this can help reduce the time to detect and respond to threats.

Overall, while IDS and IPS share similar functionality as network security systems, they have distinct differences that can affect how they are used in cybersecurity environments.

2.18   What is a security patch, and why is it important to apply them regularly?

A security patch is a software update that fixes a vulnerability in a system or an application. Vulnerabilities are weaknesses in software that can be exploited by attackers to gain unauthorized access to data, install malware, or cause other types of damage. Security patches work by addressing these vulnerabilities and closing the door to potential attacks.

Security patches are critical to maintaining the security of a system or an application. Attackers are constantly on the lookout for vulnerabilities to exploit, and when a software vulnerability is discovered, it is only a matter of time before attackers begin to use it to launch attacks. By applying security patches promptly, organizations can stay ahead of attackers and prevent exploitation before it happens.

Failing to apply security patches in a timely manner can lead to disastrous consequences. For example, the 2017 WannaCry ransomware attack infected over 200,000 devices in more than 150 countries, causing widespread disruption and damage. The attack exploited a vulnerability in Microsoft Windows for which patches had been available for several months, but many organizations had failed to apply the patches.

In addition to preventing attacks, applying security patches can also help organizations meet compliance requirements. Many regulatory standards, such as the Payment Card Industry Data Security Standard (PCI DSS) and the General Data Protection Regulation (GDPR), require organizations to keep their systems up to date with security patches.

In summary, security patches are critical to maintaining the security of a system or an application. Applying security patches promptly can help prevent attacks, minimize damage, and ensure compliance with regulatory standards.

2.19   What is a honeypot, and how is it used in cybersecurity?

A honeypot is a cybersecurity technique used to detect and analyze security threats by creating a decoy system. Honeypots are designed to look and behave like legitimate systems or applications, but are actually designed to lure attackers into revealing their tactics and techniques.

Typically, a honeypot will be a standalone system or network segment that is isolated from the rest of the IT infrastructure. It is intentionally designed to be vulnerable and easy to compromise. Once an attacker gains access to the honeypot, they will be monitored to see what types of attacks they use, what tools and techniques they employ, and what their ultimate objectives are. In many cases, honeypots will have fake data or systems that seem valuable to the attacker, but do not actually have any business value - this is intended to give the attacker a sense of accomplishment.

Honeypots are used primarily for two reasons: research and protection. From a research perspective, honeypots can be used to gather information about new and emerging threats, as well as to study the tactics and techniques of hackers. This information helps cybersecurity teams to stay ahead of the curve and develop new defenses against advanced persistent threats.

From a protection perspective, honeypots can be used to divert attackers away from critical systems and applications. By creating (fake) systems or applications that seem valuable to attackers, cyber security professionals can keep the attackers occupied and away from the real systems in the IT infrastructure.

One real-world example of honeypot usage occurred in 2010, when Google announced it had been targeted in a series of sophisticated cyber attacks dubbed "Operation Aurora." Google set up a honeypot to draw in the attackers, and was able to identify the specific IP addresses used in the attacks. This information was used to blacklist these addresses and prevent further attacks.

In summary, honeypots are a valuable tool in the cybersecurity arsenal. They provide a means for security professionals to gather intelligence on potential threats, and can be used to protect critical systems by diverting attackers away from them.

2.20   What is the role of a security incident response team (SIRT)?

The role of a Security Incident Response Team (SIRT), also known as Computer Security Incident Response Team (CSIRT) is to manage and respond to security incidents within an organization. The main goal of a SIRT is to minimize the impact of an incident and prevent it from occurring in the future.

The SIRT has several key responsibilities, which include:

1. Incident Detection: The SIRT must continuously monitor the organization's environment to identify any suspicious activity or unusual behavior.

2. Incident Response: Once an incident has been detected, the SIRT must respond quickly and effectively to contain the incident and prevent further damage. This includes isolating affected systems and devices, investigating the incident, and analyzing the impact.

3. Communication: The SIRT must communicate effectively with all relevant stakeholders, including executives, internal teams, and external parties such as law enforcement, regulators and third-party vendors. Effective communication is essential to ensure that everyone is aware of the incident, how it is being handled, and what actions they need to take.

4. Remediation: SIRT members must work to identify the root cause of the incident and take appropriate steps to remediate the issue, whether it is a security vulnerability, human error or system misconfiguration.

5. Documentation: All incidents must be thoroughly documented to aid future responses and ensure compliance with applicable regulations and policies.

Some examples of security incidents that may require the involvement of a SIRT include data breaches, malware attacks, phishing scams, network intrusions, and insider threats.

In summary, a SIRT plays a critical role in protecting an organization from cyber threats by monitoring for, detecting and responding to incidents in a timely, effective and comprehensive manner.

Chapter 3

Intermediate

3.1 What is the purpose of a risk assessment in cybersecurity?

The purpose of a risk assessment in cybersecurity is to identify, analyze, and evaluate potential risks and vulnerabilities that an organization's information systems may face. This is done in order to determine the likelihood and potential impact of a security breach, and to develop a plan to mitigate those risks.

A risk assessment typically involves four key steps:

1) Asset identification: this involves identifying all the information and technology assets that the organization has in order to understand what needs to be protected.

2) Threat identification: this involves identifying all the potential threats that could harm those assets such as hackers,

malware, physical theft, insider threats, natural disasters, etc.

3) Vulnerability assessment: this involves analyzing the vulnerabilities and weaknesses that exist within the organization's IT infrastructure that could be exploited by an attacker.

4) Risk analysis: this involves evaluating the potential impact of a successful attack, the likelihood of that attack occurring, and prioritizing risks based on their level of criticality.

The output of a risk assessment is a risk management plan that includes the recommendations of measures to be implemented to mitigate risks identified during the assessment. This may include controls such as firewalls, intrusion detection systems, access controls, and encryption, among others.

For example, a risk assessment of a financial institution may reveal that customer personal information is an asset that can be targeted by hackers, insider threats or other means. The assessment may further find that the institutions website has vulnerabilities that portends risk. The risk management plan would then suggest practical measures to address those vulnerabilities such as security patches and updates to web application firewalls to minimize website exposure, phishing awareness to guard against social engineering attacks and third-party security audits to ensure that vendors meet the security standards required by the institution.

Overall, conducting routine risk assessments and implementing the recommended measures can help an organization ensure the confidentiality, integrity, and availability of its information and technology assets, as well as comply with regulatory or legal requirements.

3.2   Can you explain the difference between penetration testing and vulnerability scanning?

Penetration testing and vulnerability scanning are two cybersecurity techniques used to identify and mitigate security risks. While the goals of both techniques are similar, there are some significant differences in their approach and scope.

Vulnerability scanning is a process of automated scanning of a system or network to identify known vulnerabilities. It involves using specialized software tools that scan the system and look for known vulnerabilities, such as missing software patches, weak passwords, or outdated software versions. Vulnerability scanning can be done remotely or locally, and it is typically an automated process that can quickly scan large environments.

On the other hand, penetration testing is more like a simulation of an attack on a network or system. It involves attempting to exploit vulnerabilities in a system or network to identify weaknesses that could compromise the security of the system. Penetration testing is conducted by skilled security professionals who use various manual and automated techniques to simulate a real-world cyber-attack scenario.

In other words, vulnerability scanning involves looking for known vulnerabilities in a system or network, while penetration testing simulates an actual cyber-attack to identify vulnerabilities that may not be visible during a vulnerability scan.

For example, a vulnerability scanner may identify that a web server has an outdated version of Apache installed, while a penetration tester may attempt to exploit a vulnerability in Apache to gain access to sensitive data or take control of the server.

In summary, vulnerability scanning is an automated process that identifies known vulnerabilities, while penetration testing is a manual process that simulates an actual cyber-attack to identify unknown vulnerabilities. Both techniques are essential for a comprehensive cybersecurity strategy and can help organizations identify and remediate security risks in their system or network.

3.3 What is a DDoS attack, and how can it be mitigated?

A Distributed Denial of Service (DDoS) attack is a type of cyber attack that aims at overwhelming a target system or network with an enormous amount of traffic or requests, thus making it inaccessible to its intended users. The attackers carry out these attacks by hijacking multiple devices, including computers, servers, and other Internet of Things (IoT) devices, to create a botnet army. These compromised devices, called "bots," then flood the target website or network with an overwhelming number of requests, significantly reducing its performance or rendering it completely inaccessible.

There are various types of DDoS attacks, including UDP flood, SYN flood, HTTP flood, and DNS amplification attacks. By exploiting known vulnerabilities within these protocols, attackers can forge IP headers or send packets that create an enormous amount of noise for a target network or system to process.

To mitigate a DDoS attack, organizations and individuals can take the following measures:

1. Invest in DDoS mitigation services: Many service providers offer DDoS mitigation services that can quickly detect and mitigate DDoS attacks. They set up advanced filters that help to stop malicious traffic without impacting legitimate traffic.

2. Increase network capacity and redundancy: An increase in network capacity can help in handling an increase in traffic triggered by attackers. Network redundancy is also essential for protecting against DDoS attacks, as it allows traffic to be diverted through multiple paths in case of a DDoS attack.

3. Firewall configuration: Organizations and individuals can use firewalls to limit the amount of traffic coming from specific sources that may be associated with the attack.

4. Blackholing: This method allows the targeted network provider to send all incoming traffic to a black hole or null route, effectively dropping all traffic before it can reach the intended destination.

5. Keep hardware and software up to date: Regularly updating hardware and software ensures that they can withstand the latest threats and exploits.

In summary, DDoS attacks pose a significant threat to organizations and individuals. Mitigation of these attacks requires a combination of technical, administrative, and physical measures to ensure network resilience against these threats.

3.4 What is the difference between black box, white box, and gray box testing?

Black box, white box, and gray box testing are different approaches to software testing that are used to find and fix potential vulnerabilities or weaknesses in software applications. Let's discuss each of these testing approaches in more detail:

1. Black Box Testing: Black box testing is a type of testing that focuses on the external behavior of software without examining the internal code. In this approach, testers will treat the software as a "black box" and only test it without any understanding of the source code. The testers do not have any knowledge of the underlying architecture, system design or code of the software. The goal is to verify that the software functions correctly as per the business requirements.

Testers performing black box testing consider the system under test from an end-user's point of view. They simulate various user behavior and interaction with the system to make sure that the software functions correctly. One of the significant advantages of black box testing is that it does not require knowledge of the internal workings of the software, so it can be performed by non-technical software testers.

One potential disadvantage of black box testing is that it may not expose all the issues in the software because it is only based on the user behavior, and some internal system problems might go unnoticed.

For example, if a tester is performing a black box test on a web application, they might input various data and try different workflows to see if the application responds as expected.

2. White Box Testing: White box testing is also known as clear box testing or structural testing. In this approach, testers are given access to the source code of the software application to test it from an internal perspective. The goal of white box testing is to verify that the software is performing as intended and that the code is logically correct.

White box testing can be performed by developers or software testers who are familiar with the internal details of the application. They use knowledge of the software code to create test cases that examine different paths of code execution. White box testing can identify bugs or programming errors in the software code that would be otherwise missed by black box testing.

For example, if a tester is performing white box testing on a software application, they would inspect the code and look for logical errors, such as undefined variables or infinite loops, and create test cases that execute those sections of code.

3. Grey Box Testing: Grey box testing is a combination of both black box and white box testing. In this approach, testers are given partial knowledge of the software code to help them in testing the software. Grey box testing can be used for testing software components that require a deeper knowledge of the application code, but the tester does not require full access to the source code.

For example, if a tester is performing grey box testing on a web application, they might have access to the source code for the login page, but not for the rest of the application. They would use this knowledge to create test cases that examine the code in the login page while simulating user behavior to explore the rest of the application.

In conclusion, the choice of testing approach may depend on the goals of the testing process, the availability of resources, and the type of software under test. Black box testing is useful when the tester has no knowledge of the internal workings of the software, white box testing is recommended when testing more complex software applications, and grey box testing is appropriate when partial access to the code is necessary for efficient testing.

3.5 Can you explain the concept of defense in depth and its importance in cybersecurity?

Defense in depth is a concept in cybersecurity that describes the practice of implementing multiple layers of security controls and measures to protect computer systems and networks from various types of cyber threats. This strategy assumes that a single layer of security may not be sufficient to prevent all possible attacks, and it aims to create a comprehensive and resilient defense system that can mitigate and manage cyber risks across all layers of an organization's infrastructure.

The importance of defense in depth in cybersecurity cannot be overstated. The multi-layered approach to security helps to reduce the likelihood of successful cyber-attacks by making it difficult for attackers to penetrate all the different security layers. This means that even if one or more layers are compromised, the remaining security defenses will still be active to help detect or block the attack and minimize the damage.

For instance, a defense in depth strategy may involve the use of several security controls, such as firewalls, intrusion detection systems (IDS), encryption, antivirus software, multi-factor authentication, vulnerability scanning, endpoint protection, and incident response plans.

Each of these defenses plays a crucial role in securing the network from a different angle, and they work together to create a robust and resilient cybersecurity posture.

Additionally, defense in depth strategies also focus on implementing security controls that address the human aspect of cybersecurity. This includes measures such as training employees on cyber hygiene, implementing security policies and procedures, conducting security awareness programs, and employee background checks.

Overall, defense in depth is an essential concept in cybersecurity because it recognizes that security threats are constantly evolving and becoming more sophisticated. By implementing a multi-layered security approach, organizations can improve their resilience to cyber threats and minimize the risks of cyberattacks.

3.6 What is a secure software development life cycle (SDLC), and why is it important?

A secure software development life cycle (SDLC) is a process that guides and provides a framework for the secure development of software. The SDLC comprises several stages, including planning, designing, developing, testing, deploying, and maintaining software. Each stage has various security controls and measures that ensure the software is developed securely and meets its intended functions.

The importance of a secure SDLC lies in the increasing threat of cyber attacks and data breaches. It is essential to integrate security early in the software development process to identify and mitigate potential vulnerabilities and threats. A secure SDLC can help organizations prevent costly security incidents and data breaches that could result in financial and reputational damages.

Moreover, a secure SDLC approach can align software development with various security standards and frameworks such as ISO 27001 and NIST. By following a secure SDLC, organizations can demonstrate compliance with such standards and frameworks, which can enhance their credibility and trust with customers and stakeholders.

Let's take an example to highlight the importance of a secure SDLC. Imagine a software development team has been tasked to develop an e-commerce platform that processes customers sensitive data such as credit card details, home addresses, and phone numbers. A secure SDLC approach would ensure that the team incorporates security measures such as encryption, access control, and secure coding practices at each stage of the SDLC. This approach can help identify and eliminate potential security risks before the software is deployed, ultimately safeguarding customer data and preventing financial and reputational losses.

3.7   What is the role of a Security Operations Center (SOC)?

A Security Operations Center (SOC) is an integral part of an organization's cybersecurity strategy. Its primary role is to monitor, analyze, detect, and respond to security incidents within an organization's environment. This includes data centers, networks, endpoints, applications, and other IT infrastructure.

The SOC is responsible for keeping the organization's data and systems secure and responding to threats in real-time. They are responsible for handling all security incidents, from detection to resolution, and for coordinating the organization's response to security threats. The SOC team is comprised of cybersecurity professionals who leverage a diverse set of skills and expertise to ensure the protection of the organization's assets.

SOCs are critical to an organization's cybersecurity posture as they act as a central hub for identifying and mitigating potential threats. They are proactive in identifying potential vulnerabilities in the organization's infrastructure and quickly responding to any incidents. Additionally, many SOCs provide valuable insights for improving security policies, procedures, and infrastructure.

Typically, a SOC consists of several key components, including a Security Information and Event Management (SIEM) system, incident response plans and procedures, threat intelligence feeds, and a team of security analysts. The SIEM system ingests logs and data from various sources, including firewalls, intrusion detection systems, and other security solutions, in order to detect anomalous behavior and potential security breaches.

SOCs leverage technology alongside human analysis to provide a holistic view of the organization's security posture. For instance, the security analysts can investigate security incidents to determine whether they represent genuine threats or false positives. In some cases, they may need to coordinate with external stakeholders, such as law enforcement agencies or regulatory bodies, to manage security incidents.

In conclusion, the SOC plays a critical role in ensuring an organization's cybersecurity posture. By monitoring, detecting, responding, and mitigating security incidents, they act as a frontline defense against cybersecurity threats. They help organizations to stay ahead of attackers and ensure that critical assets are protected.

3.8   What is the difference between hashing and encryption?

Hashing and encryption are two different techniques used in the field of cybersecurity to protect data, but they serve different purposes.

Hashing is an algorithmic process that converts plain text or data into a fixed-length value. The output of a hash function is always the same size, regardless of the size of the input data. Hashing is primarily used to create digital fingerprints of data, enabling secure data storage and transmission.

The primary purpose of hashing is to ensure the integrity of data. If two pieces of data produce the same hash value, they are identical. This makes hashing a useful tool for detecting tampering or data corruption. Hashing algorithms like MD5,

SHA-1, and SHA-256 are commonly used in password storage, message authentication, and digital signatures.

Encryption, on the other hand, is a process that converts plain text or data into ciphertext or scrambled code, making it unreadable to unauthorized users. Encryption is primarily used for confidentiality, or to protect data from unauthorized access by making it indecipherable to anyone without the decryption key.

Encryption algorithms like AES, DES, and RSA are commonly used to protect sensitive data. For example, when you visit a website and enter your credit card information, the website usually encrypts your data using SSL/TLS before transmitting it to the server to prevent eavesdropping by hackers.

In summary, while both hashing and encryption are cryptographic techniques, hashing is mainly used to ensure the integrity of data, while encryption is primarily used to ensure the confidentiality of data.

3.9 Can you explain what public key infrastructure (PKI) is and how it works?

Public Key Infrastructure (PKI) is a security protocol that is used to protect sensitive information exchanged over the internet. It is an encryption mechanism that secures data being transmitted on the internet by using a combination of public and private keys.

PKI works by using a system of digital certificates, which are issued by a trusted third-party called the Certificate Authority

(CA). These certificates contain a public key that is used to encrypt messages sent between two parties, as well as a private key that is used to decrypt the message once it has been received. In other words, the public key is used to encrypt the message and the private key is used to decrypt it, ensuring that only the intended recipient can read the message.

Here's an example of how PKI works in practice:

Suppose Alice wants to send a confidential document to Bob over the internet. In order to keep the document secure, Alice encrypts it using Bob's public key, which is included in his digital certificate. The encrypted document is then sent over the internet to Bob. When Bob receives the encrypted document, he uses his private key to decrypt it and read the confidential information.

By using PKI, Alice and Bob can protect their confidential information from unauthorized access and ensure that only the intended recipient can read it. This is especially important for sensitive transactions such as online banking, e-commerce, and other forms of electronic commerce that require secure communication.

In summary, PKI is a security protocol that uses digital certificates and a combination of public and private keys to encrypt and decrypt sensitive information sent over the internet.

3.10 What are some common types of web application vulnerabilities, such as those listed in the OWASP Top Ten?

The OWASP Top Ten is a list of the most critical web application security risks according to the Open Web Application Security Project. Some common types of web application vulnerabilities, as listed in the OWASP Top Ten, include:

1. Injection Attacks: Injection attacks occur when malicious input is inserted into an application's input fields, which can result in unauthorized access to sensitive information. A common example is SQL injection, in which an attacker injects malicious SQL code into an input field.

2. Broken Authentication and Session Management: Poorly implemented authentication and session management can allow attackers to gain unauthorized access to an application's data or functions. This can occur through weak passwords, session ID prediction, or a lack of proper logout procedures.

3. Cross-Site Scripting (XSS): XSS attacks occur when attackers inject malicious scripts into vulnerable web pages, which can then be executed by unsuspecting users. This can result in the theft of sensitive user data or the hijacking of a user's session.

4. Broken Access Controls: Broken access controls occur when an attacker gains unauthorized access to an application's functions or data through poorly implemented access controls. This can happen through URL manipulation, bypassing access control checks, or exploiting insecure direct object references.

5. Security Misconfiguration: Security misconfiguration occurs when an application is not properly configured, leaving it vulnerable to attacks. This can include things like unpatched software, weak security settings, or default logins and passwords.

6. Insecure Cryptographic Storage: Insecure cryptographic storage occurs when an application stores sensitive information in an unencrypted or poorly encrypted format. This can allow attackers to easily access and steal this sensitive data.

7. Insufficient Input Validation: Insufficient input validation occurs when an application fails to properly validate user input, which can lead to vulnerabilities such as injection attacks or buffer overflows.

8. Insecure Communications: Insecure communications occur when an application is vulnerable to man-in-the-middle attacks, eavesdropping, or other types of interception. This can occur through the use of weak encryption, improperly configured SSL/TLS, or a failure to properly authenticate users.

9. Using Components with Known Vulnerabilities: Using components with known vulnerabilities can leave an application open to attacks if those vulnerabilities are exploited. This can include using outdated or unpatched software, libraries, or frameworks.

10. Insufficient Logging and Monitoring: Insufficient logging and monitoring can make it more difficult to detect and respond to attacks, as there may not be enough information available to determine the root cause of an incident or to identify who is responsible.

These are just a few examples of web application vulnerabilities that can leave applications open to attack. It's important for developers and security professionals to understand these types of vulnerabilities in order to properly secure web applications and protect against cyber threats.

3.11 What is a cross-site scripting (XSS) attack, and how can it be prevented?

Cross-site scripting (XSS) is a type of cyber attack aimed at web applications that can allow attackers to inject malicious code into a legitimate website to steal user data, deface the website, or spread malware to other users.

There are two types of XSS attacks: stored and reflected. In stored XSS attacks, the attacker injects malicious code into a web application's database, which is then loaded onto a user's browser when they visit the page. Reflected XSS attacks, on the other hand, occur when the malicious code is reflected back to the user through a vulnerable search bar or other input field.

Preventing XSS attacks requires a multi-layered approach, including:

1. Input validation: Ensure that all input fields contain only expected values, such as alphanumeric characters or valid email addresses, and reject any unexpected input.

2. Output encoding: Encode any user-generated content before displaying it back to the user. This can involve converting special characters to their HTML entity equivalents, such as replacing < with <.

3. Content security policy (CSP): A CSP allows website own-
ers to define a set of trusted sources for scripts, stylesheets,
and other resources. This prevents attackers from injecting untrusted code into a website.

4. HTTPS: Use HTTPS to encrypt data between the server and
the user's browser, making it harder for attackers to intercept
and modify requests or responses.

5. Regular updates: Keep all web applications and software
up-to-date with the latest security patches, as vulnerabilities
are regularly discovered and exploited by attackers.

6. Browser extensions: Use browser extensions, such as No-
script or uBlock Origin, to block scripts and other potentially
malicious content from unknown sources.

By implementing these preventive measures, it is possible to
reduce the risk of a successful XSS attack and protect user
data from being compromised.

3.12   What is a SQL injection attack, and how can it be prevented?

A SQL injection attack is a type of cyber attack where an attacker exploits a vulnerability in a web application that uses
SQL (Structured Query Language) to interact with a database.
The attacker enters malicious SQL commands or code into a
form field or input area of the web application. When the application does not properly validate or escape the input, the
malicious code can manipulate the SQL statements sent to the
database and potentially compromise the security of the entire

system.

For example, let's say a web application requires users to enter a username and password to log in. The application sends a SQL query to the database to check if the entered username and password match the data stored in the database. An attacker could enter a SQL command into the username field like " 'OR 1=1;– " which would force the query to always return true, allowing the attacker to log in without a valid password.

To prevent SQL injection attacks, there are several best practices that developers can follow when creating web applications. Here are a few key steps:

1. Sanitize user input: Before using user input in SQL queries, developers should ensure that the data is safe to use. This can involve removing or encoding characters that could be used for SQL injection, such as quotes or semicolons. Sanitizing data can be done through a process called "parameterized queries" where user input is treated as a parameter rather than being directly inserted into the SQL query.

2. Limit user privileges: Web application users should only have access to the data and functionality that they need to use. This reduces the risk of an attacker being able to escalate their attack by gaining access to sensitive data or taking control of the entire system.

3. Keep software up-to-date: Regularly updating web application software, including web servers, database servers, and application frameworks, is crucial to ensuring that known vulnerabilities are patched.

4. Use a web application firewall (WAF): A WAF can help

detect and block SQL injection attacks by analyzing incoming requests and blocking any that appear to contain malicious SQL code.

By taking these steps, web application developers can minimize the risk of SQL injection vulnerabilities and help protect their systems, and their users, from malicious attacks.

3.13 What is the purpose of network segmentation in cybersecurity?

Network segmentation is the practice of dividing a network into smaller subnetworks, also known as segments or zones, to improve security and reduce the attack surface of the network. The purpose of network segmentation in cybersecurity is to limit the damage an attacker can do by separating critical assets from the rest of the network and reducing the exposure of those assets to potential threats.

By segmenting a network, an organization can group similar devices and resources together based on their level of sensitivity and trust. For example, a company might create separate segments for production servers, employee workstations, and guest devices. Each of these segments can have its own set of security controls and access restrictions based on the specific needs of that segment.

Network segmentation offers several benefits in terms of cybersecurity. Here are some of the most important ones:

1. Minimizes the impact of a successful attack: If an attacker gains access to one segment of a network, network segmenta-

tion can prevent them from moving laterally to other segments. This can limit the scope of a successful attack and prevent the attacker from accessing critical resources.

2. Improves compliance: Many security regulations require network segmentation, including HIPAA and PCI DSS. By implementing network segmentation, an organization can better meet compliance requirements and avoid costly fines and legal fees.

3. Reduces attack surface: A segmented network means that there are fewer devices and resources exposed to potential threats. This makes it easier for security teams to monitor the network and detect unusual activity.

4. Enables better security controls: With network segmentation, it is easier to implement targeted security controls for each segment of the network. For example, critical assets can be protected with stronger access controls and monitoring than less sensitive resources.

5. Facilitates easier management: A segmented network usually means that resources are more organized and easier to manage. This can help IT staff better understand the network and quickly troubleshoot any issues that arise.

Overall, network segmentation is a critical component of a comprehensive cybersecurity strategy. By separating resources and limiting access to sensitive information, organizations can significantly reduce their exposure to cyber threats and improve their ability to respond to security incidents.

3.14 Can you explain the concepts of data classification and data handling in a security context?

In the context of cybersecurity, data classification is the process of identifying the sensitivity and value of data and organizing it into different categories based on those parameters. The aim of data classification is to provide a framework for managing and protecting data according to its importance, thus ensuring adequate measures are put in place to safeguard it against unauthorized access, theft, modification or loss.

There are typically four main levels of classification, including:

1. Public: This category includes data that is available to the public and poses no risk to the organization if it is disclosed. Examples of such data include press releases or marketing collateral.

2. Internal Use: This category consists of data that is not for public consumption but is not sensitive enough to require strict protection. Examples of such data include internal policies, procedures, and memos.

3. Confidential: This category includes data that is sensitive to the organization and could harm the organization if improperly disclosed. Examples of such data include customer data, financial information, and intellectual property.

4. Top Secret: This category includes data that is extremely sensitive and could potentially cause catastrophic consequences if it fell into the wrong hands. Examples of such data include government or law enforcement classified information, military

secrets, and trade secrets.

Data handling, on the other hand, refers to how data should be stored, accessed, and transmitted, based on its classification level. The primary goal of data handling is to ensure that data is kept secure, both on and off the network.

Here are some best practices for handling data:

1. Security Protocols: All sensitive data should be encrypted to protect it from being accessed by unauthorized users.

2. Access Controls: Internal access controls should be put in place to ensure that only those authorized to access the data can do so.

3. Network Security: The network should be secured using firewalls, intrusion detection systems, and other tools to ensure that sensitive data is not accessed externally.

4. Secure Disposal: Sensitive data should be disposed of in a secure way, such as shredding, wiping or destroying hard disks, or using data disposal methods that follow data regulatory standards such as DISA and NIST.

Overall, it's essential to understand the importance of data classification and handling in a security context because it helps organizations identify their most important assets and ensures that appropriate protection measures are put in place to safeguard them properly.

3.15   What is the difference between network-based and host-based security solutions?

Network-based and host-based security solutions are two main types of cybersecurity defenses that protect computer networks and devices. The main difference between them lies in the location where the security measures are implemented and enforced.

Network-based security solutions operate at the network level and protect the entire network infrastructure. They are typically implemented using specialized hardware and software tools, such as firewalls, intrusion detection and prevention systems, and network sandboxes. Network security solutions are designed to monitor and analyze network traffic, identify potential threats, and block malicious activities before they reach the endpoints. Using network-based security solutions, administrators can set and enforce security policies and configure access controls to regulate who can access network resources and from where.

On the other hand, host-based security solutions operate at the individual device level, protecting the endpoints and the applications running on them. These solutions are typically implemented as software agents installed on individual desktops, servers, laptops, and smartphones. Host-based security solutions use various techniques to monitor the device's activities, detect and block malware, and enforce security policies. They also include features such as antivirus and anti-malware protection, intrusion detection and prevention, data loss prevention, and host-based firewalls.

Host-based security solutions are particularly effective at protecting endpoints that connect to a network remotely or outside the organization's perimeter. They can detect and block malware that may have evaded network security protections and can monitor and control user activities on the device.

In summary, network-based security solutions and host-based security solutions both serve different purposes, but they complement each other in terms of providing cyber threat protection. Network-based security solutions protect a network's perimeter and infrastructure, while host-based security solutions protect the endpoints and the applications running on them. Together, they provide a more comprehensive security posture and help organizations defend against advanced cyber threats.

3.16 What is a Zero Trust security model, and why is it important?

The Zero Trust security model is a paradigm for network security that proposes that organizations should not automatically trust any user, device, or endpoint that attempts to access their network. Instead, every user or device should be verified and authenticated before being granted access to network resources. This is based on the principle of "never trust, always verify."

Zero Trust is important because traditional network security models assume that once a user is within the firewall, they can be trusted to access all resources within that network. This approach has proved to be ineffective in preventing malicious attacks from inside or outside of the network, particularly with the growth of remote workforces and mobile devices accessing corporate resources.

Zero Trust model addresses these issues by implementing strict access controls and verification measures at every possible layer of the network. This means that users and devices are continuously authenticated before access is granted. This approach limits the amount of access and control granted to each user or device based on security need-to-know and emphasizes an identity-based approach to security, rather than trying to protect network perimeters.

Some examples of Zero Trust security model implementation include multi-factor authentication (MFA), privileged access management (PAM), least privilege access control, identity and access management (IAM), and network segmentation.

Benefits of implementing the Zero Trust model in an organization include stronger security posture, better detection, and prevention of attacks, increased visibility into network activity, and compliance with regulatory requirements.

3.17 Can you explain the role of security information and event management (SIEM) systems in cybersecurity?

Security Information and Event Management (SIEM) systems play a crucial role in cybersecurity by helping organizations detect and respond to cyber threats in real-time. Specifically, SIEM systems collect and analyze security-related data from various sources like servers, network devices, and applications to identify potential threats and suspicious activities.

SIEM systems provide a centralized platform to collect, analyze, and correlate data from different sources to give a holistic view of an organization's security posture. This holistic view allows security teams to identify and respond to security incidents across the entire environment, rather than just a few isolated systems.

Moreover, SIEM systems offer advanced threat detection capabilities with the help of AI and machine learning algorithms. They are able to detect patterns of suspicious behavior that may indicate the presence of a malicious actor, and can raise an alert in real-time to security teams.

In addition to threat detection and alerting, SIEM systems also provide other security benefits. For example, they help organizations meet regulatory compliance requirements by providing detailed logging and auditing capabilities, and they enable security teams to conduct forensic investigations after an attack has occurred.

Overall, SIEM systems play an important role in cybersecurity by helping organizations detect and respond to potential threats and attacks in real-time, thereby reducing the risk of data breaches and other cyber incidents.

3.18   What is the concept of threat intelligence, and how is it used in cybersecurity?

Threat intelligence is the process of gathering, analyzing, and sharing information about potential and existing cyber threats.

It involves collecting data from various sources, including the dark web, open-source intelligence, social media, and other internal and external sources. The purpose of threat intelligence is to help organizations identify and mitigate potential security threats proactively.

In cybersecurity, threat intelligence is a critical component of an organization's security strategy. It helps security teams to stay ahead of emerging and evolving threats by providing contextual information about potential attacks, including indicators of compromise (IOCs), cybercriminals, their tactics, techniques, and procedures (TTPs), malicious software, and vulnerabilities, among others. With this information, security teams can develop effective mitigation strategies, analyze and identify patterns, and respond promptly to emerging threats before they cause any damage.

There are different types of threat intelligence, including tactical, strategic, and operational intelligence. Tactical intelligence focuses on detailed information about an immediate threat, such as a targeted attack on an organization. Strategic intelligence, on the other hand, provides insights into long-term trends or campaigns, such as advanced persistent threats (APTs). Operational intelligence provides real-time information about security events, including alerts and incidents.

Threat intelligence is used in cybersecurity to achieve various goals, including:

1. Threat detection: By analyzing threat intelligence data, security teams can identify patterns and indicators of potential threats that help to detect and respond to threats in real-time.

2. Risk management: Threat intelligence helps organizations

to identify and prioritize critical assets that are likely to be targeted and assess their risk exposure, allowing them to allocate resources effectively.

3. Incident response: Threat intelligence helps to improve incident response by providing contextual information about threats and attackers, enabling teams to respond more effectively and efficiently to potential incidents.

4. Vulnerability management: Threat intelligence provides information about vulnerabilities that enable security teams to patch or update applications and systems promptly, reducing the risk of exploitation.

In conclusion, threat intelligence is a vital component of cybersecurity that provides organizations with the necessary information to stay ahead of emerging threats. It plays a critical role in threat detection, risk management, incident response, and vulnerability management.

3.19 What are some common types of cloud security threats, and how can they be mitigated?

Cloud computing has revolutionized the way we store, process, and manage data. However, as with any technology, it comes with its own set of security threats. Here are some common types of cloud security threats and how to mitigate them:

1. Data Breaches - Data breaches occur when unauthorized individuals gain access to sensitive data. Cloud providers use

a shared responsibility model which means both the provider and the customer are responsible for protecting the data. To mitigate data breaches, customers should encrypt sensitive data before storing it in the cloud, use strong authentication methods, and monitor access to data.

2. Insider Threats - Insider threats are attacks that originate from within an organization. The threat could come from an employee, a contractor, or any other individual with authorized access to the cloud. To mitigate insider threats, customers should implement access controls, use encryption to protect data, and monitor activity on the cloud platform.

3. Denial-of-Service (DoS) Attacks DoS attacks can disrupt access to cloud resources, causing them to become unavailable to legitimate users. To mitigate DoS attacks, customers should implement network security controls, use service providers with DoS protection, and use load balancing technologies to distribute traffic evenly.

4. Malware - Malware is malicious software that can infect cloud systems and cause damage. To mitigate malware risks, customers should use anti-virus software, encrypt sensitive data, and limit access to files through user permissions.

5. Account Hijacking - Account hijacking occurs when criminals gain access to a user's cloud account. To mitigate the risk of account hijacking, customers should use strong passwords, enable multi-factor authentication, and have a process for revoking access to accounts.

In summary, cloud security threats are a concern for any organization using cloud services. Customers can mitigate these threats by using strong access controls, encryption, multi-factor authentication, and monitoring activity. Additionally, customers should work with their cloud provider to understand their shared responsibility model and implement the necessary security controls to protect sensitive data.

3.20 What is the difference between security orchestration, automation, and response (SOAR) and SIEM?

Both Security Orchestration, Automation and Response (SOAR) and Security Information and Event Management (SIEM) were created to help organizations detect, respond to, and contain cyber threats. However, there are some key differences between the two technologies.

SIEM systems are designed to collect and analyze data from various sources in real-time. They typically use rule-based analysis and correlation to identify threats, generate alerts for security teams, and store log data for forensic purposes. SIEM systems require human operators to investigate and respond to alerts manually.

SOAR, on the other hand, extends the capabilities of SIEM systems by automating the response process to detected threats. They leverage machine learning and artificial intelligence (AI) to analyze security events and dynamically orchestrate and automate threat responses. SOAR tools work by integrating with an organizations existing security technologies and workflows to facilitate faster incident response and make better use of security resources.

Here are some of the key differences between SOAR and SIEM:

1. Automation: SIEM systems are designed to generate alerts and reports, but they don't take action on their own. SOAR tools automate the threat response process, freeing up human analysts to focus on more complex issues.

2. Integration: SIEM systems collect log data from disparate sources and correlate it for easy analysis, while SOAR tools integrate with a broader range of security technologies such as firewalls, endpoint detection, and response (EDR) systems, to name a few.

3. Incident response: SIEM systems provide a starting point for a security team to start investigating, while SOAR solutions provide them with a roadmap for faster remediation by automating the incident response process.

4. Complexity: SIEM systems can be complex to set up, configure, and maintain. They may require extensive training to use effectively, while SOAR tools can provide out-of-the-box automation solutions, which can significantly simplify operations.

In summary, both SOAR and SIEM solutions are critical components of a modern cybersecurity strategy, but they serve different roles. SIEM solutions are primarily detection and alerting tools while SOAR provides advanced automation and orchestration of the incident response process to take the appropriate steps against detected threats.

Chapter 4

Advanced

4.1 Can you describe the main steps in the incident response process?

The incident response process consists of several main steps that should be followed in order to effectively respond to any cybersecurity incident. Those steps are:

1. Preparation: Preparation is a critical step that involves setting up policies, procedures, and protocols to ensure the proper handling of cybersecurity incidents. It includes creating incident management teams, defining roles and responsibilities, and ensuring that the necessary technology and tools are available to detect and respond to incidents. It's essentially the step where the organization sets the groundwork for what it will do when an incident occurs.

2. Identification: The next step is to identify the incident.

This can be done through various means like automated tools or manual monitoring. Organizations use tools such as security information and event management (SIEM) systems to monitor their networks in real-time, looking for signs of malicious activities or vulnerabilities. Additionally, users and employees can report any suspicious activity via a ticketing or incident reporting system.

3. Containment: Once the incident is identified, the primary goal of the organization is to try to contain it as quickly as possible to prevent further damage. This involves isolating affected systems, shutting down network connections, or even severing certain parts of the network from the rest of the organization. The goal of containment is to prevent the spread of malware or other malicious activity, minimize data loss, and restore business operations.

4. Investigation: This step involves investigating the incident to determine the scope, impact, and root cause of the breach. It involves gathering evidence, and to do that the organization must analyze logs, packet captures, or memory images. The goal of this phase is to learn as much as possible about what happened so that the organization can make informed decisions about how to proceed and prevent the same incident from happening again in the future.

5. Response: After a thorough investigation, the organization must decide on the best response to the incident depending on its severity, root cause, and potential impact. This step may involve restoring systems from backups, patching vulnerabilities, or changing security configurations. It may also involve notifying regulators, law enforcement or other stakeholders depending on the nature of the incident.

6. Recovery: The final step involves returning the organization to its normal operating state. This includes restoring affected systems, conducting post-incident reviews to identify any areas for improvement, and updating the incident response plan based on the lessons learned from the incident.

Overall, an effective incident response plan is critical to minimizing the impact of a cybersecurity incident on an organization. Implementing best practices and following a structured approach ensures an organization can handle an incident quickly, effectively and with as little disruption to its operations as possible.

4.2 What is the role of digital forensics in cybersecurity, and what are some common forensic techniques?

Digital forensics plays a crucial role in cybersecurity as it involves the identification, preservation, analysis, and presentation of digital evidence to understand the nature of cybercrime, identify the perpetrators, and prevent similar incidents from happening in the future. Cybercrime investigations are heavily reliant on digital forensic techniques, such as the recovery of deleted data, analysis of network traffic and malware, and tracking of user activity.

Some common forensic techniques used in cybersecurity investigations include:

1. Disk Imaging: This involves creating an exact copy of a device's hard drive or memory for analysis. Disk imaging is

essential in investigations as it preserves the digital evidence, prevents further tampering, and enables investigators to analyze the data without altering the original source.

2. Network Forensics: This involves capturing and analyzing network traffic to identify suspicious patterns or behaviors, such as unauthorized access, information theft, or malware activity. Network forensic techniques help investigators to trace the source of attacks, identify the affected systems, and prevent future security breaches.

3. Memory Forensics: This involves analyzing the volatile memory of a device to gather evidence of system activities, such as running processes, network connections, user activities, and open files. Memory forensics techniques are beneficial in detecting advanced persistent threats (APTs), which are designed to evade traditional forms of cybersecurity.

4. Malware Analysis: This involves analyzing and reverse engineering malicious code to understand its behavior, purpose, and potential impact on an organization. Malware analysis is critical in identifying and responding to threats such as ransomware, spyware, and viruses.

5. Data Recovery: This involves extracting data from damaged, deleted or corrupted storage devices such as hard drives, USB drives, and memory cards. Data recovery can be crucial in investigations where evidence has been tampered with, erased, or encrypted.

In conclusion, digital forensics is an essential component of cybersecurity, and its techniques are essential in identifying and responding to cybersecurity incidents. The use of forensic techniques allows investigators to analyze the digital evidence to understand the nature of the offense committed, the perpetrator, and prevent similar incidents from reoccurring.

4.3 How do advanced persistent threats (APTs) differ from other types of cyberattacks?

Advanced persistent threats (APTs) are a type of cyberattack that is typically more sophisticated, targeted, and persistent than other types of attacks. APTs differ from other types of cyberattacks in several key ways:

1. Targeted: APTs are specifically targeted at a particular organization or individual. Attackers invest significant time and resources to gather information about the target and develop a tailored attack strategy. This means that the attack is likely to be more successful in achieving the attacker's goals.

2. Covert: APTs are designed to remain undetected for as long as possible. Attackers will typically use techniques such as social engineering, spear-phishing, or other means of circumventing traditional security controls to gain access to the target's network.

3. Persistence: APTs are designed to remain in the target's network for an extended period, sometimes months or even years. Attackers will use various means to maintain their control, such as hiding their presence, using multiple backdoors, and constantly changing their tactics to avoid detection.

4. Advanced Techniques: APTs often use advanced techniques,

such as zero-day exploits, advanced malware or ransomware, and other advanced tactics. Attackers will tailor their attack strategy to the target's specific security controls and use techniques that are difficult to detect or mitigate.

5. Motive: APTs are typically carried out by well-funded, state-sponsored or criminal groups with specific motives. These motives can include stealing valuable data, disrupting the target's operations, or espionage.

For example, the Target data breach in 2013 was an example of an APT attack. Attackers stole payment card data from Target's point-of-sale systems, which had been compromised via a remote access tool used by Target's HVAC contractor. The attackers remained undetected for months, and the attack was highly targeted and sophisticated, involving multiple stages and tactics to extract the data.

In summary, APTs are typically more complex, targeted, and persistent than other types of cyberattacks. They require a tailored approach that uses advanced techniques to remain undetected and achieve the attacker's objectives.

4.4   Can you explain the concept of data loss prevention (DLP) and its importance in an organization?

Data loss prevention (DLP) is a set of tools and processes that are designed to prevent the loss, theft, or exposure of sensitive data. Sensitive data can include trade secrets, financial information, personally identifiable information (PII), and other confidential information that could be harmful to an organization or its customers if it falls into the wrong hands.

DLP works by analyzing data as it moves through an organization's networks, devices, and systems. It looks for patterns that indicate sensitive data, such as credit card numbers or social security numbers, and applies rules to prevent that data from leaving the organization unauthorized. This can include blocking emails that contain sensitive data, preventing employees from uploading sensitive data to cloud storage, or monitoring suspicious activity that could indicate a data breach.

There are several reasons why DLP is important in an organization:

1. Compliance: Many organizations are subject to data protection regulations, such as GDPR or HIPAA, which require them to safeguard sensitive data. DLP can help organizations meet these compliance requirements by preventing data loss and demonstrating to regulatory bodies that they have effective data protection policies and procedures in place.

2. Business continuity: Losing sensitive data can be catastrophic for organizations, leading to reputational damage, loss of customer trust, and financial penalties. DLP helps organizations to safeguard their sensitive data and maintain business continuity in the event of a data breach.

3. Competitive advantage: Organizations that can demonstrate a strong commitment to data protection are more likely to win business from customers who value privacy and security. By implementing DLP, organizations can differentiate themselves from their competitors and build trust with their customers.

To give an example, let's say an organization processes credit card payments for its customers. If sensitive credit card data were to be compromised through a data breach, the organization could face significant financial penalties, lose revenue due to reputational damage, and suffer a loss of customer trust. By implementing DLP, the organization could prevent credit card data from leaving the organization unauthorized, significantly reducing the risk of a data breach and protecting the organization from the potential consequences.

4.5   What are some common techniques used in reverse engineering malware?

Reverse engineering is a process of analyzing software to understand its code and functionality. In the case of malware, reverse engineering is used to uncover how the malware operates, identify its capabilities and any vulnerabilities it may exploit. Here are some common techniques that are used in reverse engineering malware:

1. Dynamic Analysis: Dynamic analysis involves executing the malware in a controlled environment such as a virtual machine or sandbox. The aim is to observe the malwares behavior when it interacts with the system, what it does and how it does it. Analyzing a malware sample under a debugger allows the security professional to step into the code execution to observe changes to memory, execution flow and system calls. This technique can help identify its purpose, the type of malware, and the command and control (C2) servers it is communicating with.

2. Static Analysis: Static analysis examines the code without

executing it. This is done by disassembling or decompiling the malware, and examining its structure, function calls and dependencies. Static analysis can provide important information about the malwares capabilities and purpose, such as whether it is designed to run as a rootkit or whether it has network communication capabilities. This technique is appropriate if one need values that remain constant overtime or if the malware is designed to self-destruct once triggered.

3. Memory Forensics: Memory forensics is the process of analyzing the memory contents of a machine to identify the behavior of a malware sample that is currently running in memory. Malware often uses memory to hide itself or its activity, and memory analysis can help identify the location of the malware in memory, the system calls it makes, the data structures it creates, and the network activity it generates.

4. Code Reconstruction: Code Reconstruction involves reconstructing or rebuilding the source code of malware from disassembled binaries. This technique can help reverse engineers understand the behavior of a complex malware family as well as assist with software fixes and improvements.

5. Behavioral Analysis: Behavioral analysis is a comprehensive test that runs a malware sample in a test environment, and monitors all changes, files and registry modifications, and network activity. Using this technique, the security professional can obtain a comprehensive understanding of how the malware interacts with the operating system and the rest of the network.

In conclusion, reverse engineering malware is an essential process for cybersecurity professionals, and these five common techniques can be used to analyze and understand the functionality of malware. By combining these techniques with threat intelligence data, threat hunters can better identify and respond to attacks, prevent future attacks and enhance overall cybersecurity.

4.6   What is the difference between containerization and virtualization, and how do they relate to cybersecurity?

Containerization and virtualization are two different technologies used in the world of cybersecurity to improve agility, portability, and security of software systems. Although they serve similar purposes, they have some fundamental differences in how they are implemented and how they can be used to enhance security.

Virtualization is a method of creating multiple virtual machines (VMs) on a single physical server or cloud platform. Each VM can run its own operating system (OS), applications, and services, mimicking a complete physical computing environment. VMs are isolated from each other, and they have their own set of hardware resources, including CPU, memory, storage, and network interfaces. This allows different tasks to be performed on a single physical machine, which increases resource utilization and reduces hardware costs, while providing security and isolation for applications. VMs can be used in a variety of cyber security scenarios, including secure testing and development, malware sandboxing, and penetration testing.

On the other hand, containerization is a lightweight method of virtualization that allows multiple isolated instances of an application to run on a single operating system kernel. Instead of creating a complete virtual machine, containers use the host operating system's kernel to provide resource isolation and process separation. Containers contain only the application and its dependencies, making them smaller, faster, and more efficient compared to VMs. They also provide a consistent and portable environment for deploying applications, which makes them ideal for security, scalability, and agility. Containerization is often used in cybersecurity to improve application security and reduce attack surfaces by isolating applications and their dependencies from the underlying OS.

From a security perspective, both virtualization and containerization can be used to isolate and secure applications, but they have different security implications. VMs are more secure because they provide complete isolation from the host system, which can provide an additional layer of protection from attacks on the host OS. However, VMs require more resources and are slower to create and deploy. Containers, on the other hand, are faster and more lightweight, but they share the operating system kernel with the host OS, which can present more security risks. Containers require additional security measures to ensure that they are isolated and secured from the host system, such as secure image signing, runtime security policies, and network segmentation.

In summary, both containerization and virtualization are important technologies for improving cybersecurity, providing secure and efficient environments for running applications. Container technology is preferred over traditional virtualization in scenarios where portability, agility and security of application is prime concern.

4.7 What are the main components of a security policy, and why is it important for an organization?

A security policy is a document that outlines the guidelines and rules of an organization regarding the protection of its critical assets and information from unauthorized access, use, or disclosure. It provides a baseline for establishing and maintaining a secure and compliant environment in which an organization can operate. The main components of a security policy include:

1. Purpose statement- This defines the purpose of the document and sets the tone for the overall policy.

2. Scope statement- This outlines the group or area to which the policy applies, and defines what it covers.

3. Roles and responsibilities- The policy should assign specific roles and responsibilities to individuals or groups for the implementation of security controls, monitoring, and reporting of security incidents.

4. Security controls- The policy should identify the specific security controls used to protect the organization's assets and information such as access controls, firewalls, endpoint protection, and encryption.

5. Incident response and reporting procedures- The policy should outline the process for responding to security incidents, including the steps to be taken, the necessary notifications, and the reporting requirements.

6. Compliance requirements- The policy should identify any

compliance requirements that the organization must meet, such as regulatory or legal requirements.

Having a comprehensive security policy is crucial for any organization for several reasons:

1. Protection of valuable assets- A security policy helps to safeguard an organization's critical assets from theft, loss, or damage.

2. Risk mitigation- A policy helps identify risks and develop adequate controls to minimize potential damages.

3. Regulatory compliance- Having a policy that meets regulatory or legal requirements ensures that the organization is compliant with the law, and avoids fines, legal penalties, or reputational damage.

4. Consistency- A policy provides consistency in the way that employees and stakeholders handle sensitive data by ensuring a standard approach is taken to its care and maintenance.

5. Increased trust and confidence- A policy that is well-communicated and adhered to by every person within the organization, promotes trust, and confidence with clients, vendors, and partners that expect accountability.

Overall, a security policy is crucial for securing the systems, information, and assets that are essential to an organization's operation. It is a fundamental component of the security posture for any organization, and forms the basis for all other security control procedures.

4.8   Can you discuss the role of threat modeling in secure software design?

Threat modeling is the process of systematically identifying and evaluating potential security threats to a system, application, or network. It plays a critical role in secure software design by allowing developers to identify potential security risks early in the software development lifecycle and to design mitigations to these risks.

The following are some of the benefits of threat modeling in secure software design:

1. Identifying Security Risks: Threat modeling helps in identifying potential security risks to an application or system. This information is critical for developers to be able to design effective security controls to mitigate such risks.

2. Prioritizing Security Controls: Based on the potential security risks identified during the threat modeling process, the team can prioritize and decide on the most important security features to be implemented first.

3. Cost Savings: Identifying security risks early in the software development process is significantly less costly than dealing with security vulnerabilities detected in the production phase. Threat modeling helps in identifying and addressing potential security threats before they are exploited.

4. Compliance and Certification: Compliance with industry security standards such as PCI DSS, HIPAA, or ISO 27001 require the implementation of adequate security controls. Threat modeling can help in identifying and addressing such require-

ments.

5. Improving Awareness: Threat modeling helps in raising awareness of security issues among developers and stakeholders. This helps in improving the overall security culture of the organization and reducing security incidents.

Threat modeling involves several steps which can vary depending upon the methodology that is chosen. Below are some of the general steps that are involved:

- 1. Identify the scope and boundaries (e.g., the system or application to be analyzed)

- 2. Identify threats and potential attack vectors (e.g., malicious actors, malware, vulnerabilities)

- 3. Assess the likelihood and impact of each threat, considering factors such as the value of the asset being targeted, the skill level of the attacker, and the potential impact if the attack succeeds.

- 4. Prioritize the risks: Based on the findings, prioritize the potential risks of attack

- 5. Identify the most effective controls / mitigation strategies to address each prioritized risk.

The goal of threat modeling is to identify potential security risks early in the software development process and to design mitigating controls that can help reduce the overall risk of security incidents. By following proper threat modeling guidelines, developers can ensure that security issues are addressed before they become a problem, saving organizations time, money, and other valuable resources.

4.9 How can organizations ensure compliance with data protection and privacy regulations such as GDPR and CCPA?

Organizations can ensure compliance with data protection and privacy regulations such as GDPR and CCPA by taking the following steps:

1. Conduct a Privacy Impact Assessment (PIA): Conduct a PIA to identify personal data and sensitive information that needs to be protected, the risks and threats to that data, how the data is collected, processed, and stored, and what measures should be put in place to protect it.

2. Implement Privacy by Design: Implement privacy by design principles that foresee privacy compliance requirements at the early stages of product development, software development, and project planning.

3. Implement data minimization techniques: Implement techniques such as data minimization to collect only the data that is necessary and relevant to the purpose for which it is intended.

4. Implement user consent management: Implement user consent management procedures that require clear affirmative consent before data is collected, processed, or shared.

5. Ensure data subject rights: Ensure that data subjects have the right to access, correct, and delete their personal data.

6. Ensure data protection and security: Implement measures to protect personal data during processing, storage, and trans-

mission, such as encryption, access controls, and monitoring.

7. Implement ongoing monitoring and auditing: Implement ongoing monitoring and auditing to ensure that compliance with data protection regulations and privacy policies is maintained over time.

8. Train employees and contractors: Train employees and contractors to understand their roles and responsibilities in maintaining data protection and privacy compliance.

An example of this could include a healthcare organization that has to comply with CCPA and GDPR regulations. They could conduct a PIA to identify personal data they are collecting and processing, implement measures such as encryption and access controls to protect the sensitive information, allow users to modify their information, and provide GDPR and CCPA training to employees and contractors on their roles in maintaining these regulations. By implementing these measures, the organization complies with data protection and privacy regulations while protecting confidential data.

4.10 What are some challenges in securing the Internet of Things (IoT) and how can they be addressed?

The Internet of Things (IoT) refers to a network of physical devices, vehicles, and other items that are embedded with sensors, connectivity, and software that enable them to collect and exchange data over the internet. IoT devices have become increasingly popular, with estimates indicating that there will be over 75 billion of these devices by the end of 2025. However, securing these devices poses a significant challenge due to various factors, including:

1. Limited processing power and memory: Most IoT devices have limited processing power and memory, which makes it difficult to install and run security software. This makes them vulnerable to attacks, as they are not equipped to defend against them.

2. Diverse communication protocols: IoT devices use different communication protocols, such as Wi-Fi, Bluetooth, and Zigbee. Each protocol has its unique security challenges, and different devices may use different connections for communication. This makes it challenging to implement standardized security measures.

3. Complex supply chains: IoT devices are manufactured by different vendors and suppliers, and each part of an IoT device may come from a different source. This makes it challenging to ensure the security of every component.

4. Lack of firmware updates: Many IoT devices are not designed with firmware updates in mind. This means that once a vulnerability is identified, it may be challenging or even impossible to fix.

To address these challenges, several measures can be put in place, such as:

1. Implementing strong authentication and access controls: IoT devices should be designed with strong authentication mechanisms to ensure that only authorized users can access the device.

2. Encrypting communication: IoT devices should use end-to-

end encryption to prevent unauthorized access and eavesdropping.

3. Conducting regular software updates: IoT vendors should regularly release software updates to patch vulnerabilities and fix security issues.

4. Firewalls and VPNs: Using firewall protection and VPNs can provide additional security for IoT devices by blocking unauthorized traffic.

5. Standardizing security protocols: The development of standardized security protocols can make it easier to secure IoT devices effectively.

6. Promoting security awareness: Educating consumers and businesses about the importance of IoT security and best practices can raise awareness and promote adherence to secure practices.

In summary, securing the IoT requires a multi-layered approach because different devices have different security challenges. By implementing a combination of these measures, we can address the challenges of securing IoT devices and help reduce the risk of security breaches.

4.11   What is a security maturity model, and how can it be used to improve an organization's cybersecurity posture?

A security maturity model is a framework that helps organizations understand and measure their overall security posture. It allows organizations to assess their current security capabilities, identify gaps and weaknesses, and develop a plan for improving their security over time.

Typically, a security maturity model is designed as a progression of stages or levels, with each level representing an increasing level of maturity and capability. These levels are typically defined based on specific security controls and practices that the organization should have in place at each level.

For example, a common security maturity model used in the industry is the Capability Maturity Model Integration (CMMI) Security model. This model defines five levels of security maturity, ranging from Level 1 - Initial (ad hoc and chaotic) to Level 5 - Optimizing (continuous improvement and innovation).

By using a security maturity model, organizations can assess their current level of security maturity and identify areas for improvement. They can then develop a roadmap for increasing their security maturity over time, such as implementing new security controls, improving existing processes, or investing in new security technologies.

The benefit of using a security maturity model is that it allows organizations to take a proactive approach to security, rather than simply reacting to security incidents as they occur. It also helps organizations prioritize their security initiatives based on their business needs and risk profile.

For example, a large financial institution may prioritize achieving Level 5 maturity, as they are a high-risk target for cyberattacks and require the latest and most advanced security capabilities. On the other hand, a small business may focus on achieving Level 2 maturity, as they have limited resources and need to prioritize basic security practices such as access management and patching.

In summary, a security maturity model provides organizations with a structured approach to improving their security posture. It helps organizations understand their current capabilities, identify areas for improvement, and prioritize security initiatives to protect against cyber threats.

4.12 What is the concept of security analytics, and how does it differ from traditional SIEM?

Security analytics is the process of using analytics tools and techniques to analyze data collected from various sources to detect security threats, identify patterns, and respond efficiently to incidents. It is an advanced approach to security management that goes beyond traditional security operations and event management (SIEM) tools.

The traditional SIEM approach involves the collection of event logs from various sources such as network devices, servers, and endpoints, and then analyzes these logs to detect security incidents. While SIEMs offer a great deal of functionality, they tend to have limitations that prevent them from detecting sophisticated and advanced threats.

On the other hand, security analytics can take a more proactive and comprehensive approach to threat detection by utilizing Machine Learning (ML) algorithms and other techniques to identify patterns or anomalous behavior that may indicate the presence of a threat. Security analytics solutions can process, analyze, and correlate vast amounts of data from multiple sources, often in real-time, allowing analysts to identify potential threats and respond quickly.

For instance, a security analytics tool might analyze user behavior, network traffic, and endpoint activity to detect unusual activity or suspicious patterns indicative of advanced persistent threats (APTs). By examining historical data and contextual information in real-time, analysts can uncover hidden threats before they cause any significant harm.

In summary, security analytics goes beyond traditional SIEM by providing a more comprehensive and proactive approach to analyzing data to identify potential threats. It leverages ML, big data technology, and data visualization to detect and respond to security threats faster and with greater accuracy.

4.13   How can machine learning and artificial intelligence be applied to cybersecurity?

Machine learning and artificial intelligence (AI) have become powerful tools in the cybersecurity industry, as they can automate and enhance threat detection, prevention and response capabilities. Here are some examples of how machine learning and AI can be applied to cybersecurity:

1. Threat detection: With the use of machine learning algorithms, cybersecurity experts can train their systems to detect and prevent threats by analyzing patterns and data from past incidents. Machine learning algorithms can identify anomalies in data traffic and flag potential threats before they cause harm. For example, intrusion detection systems (IDS) and intrusion prevention systems (IPS) are capable of using machine learning to detect and prevent hacking, phishing, ransomware and other types of security threats.

2. Malware detection: Machine learning algorithms can also be used to detect malware, including viruses, trojans, worms and ransomware. By analyzing patterns and behavior of known malware, machine learning systems can identify and quarantine malicious software before it can cause damage. The use of machine learning in malware detection has become critical as malware authors continue to develop more sophisticated and evasive tactics to evade traditional antivirus software.

3. Cybersecurity automation: Machine learning and AI tools can automate several cybersecurity tasks, including prevention, detection, and response, freeing up resources for cybersecurity teams to focus on more critical and complex tasks. For exam-

ple, autonomous response systems can detect and stop attacks without human intervention, reducing the response time and speeding up the incident resolution.

4. User behavior analysis: Machine learning algorithms can be applied to user activity data to detect and prevent insider threats such as data exfiltration and unauthorized access. By analyzing user behavior patterns and correlating them with past incidents, machine learning systems can flag potentially risky user behavior that requires further investigation.

In conclusion, machine learning and AI offer significant potential for enhancing cybersecurity by adding a layer of automation, detecting and preventing security threats, and providing faster and more accurate incident response. However, it is essential to ensure the algorithms are constantly updated and reviewed to prevent potential vulnerabilities to the cybersecurity systems.

4.14   What is the role of identity and access management (IAM) in an organization's security strategy?

Identity and access management (IAM) is a critical component of an organization's security strategy. IAM is the art and science of managing digital identities and the access rights of individuals to an organization's resources. This includes controlling access to physical locations, databases, applications, systems, and networks. IAM helps organizations establish a secure and seamless network by addressing who has access to what data and applications, and what they can do with it.

Here are some examples of the role played by IAM in an organization's security strategy:

1.   Access Control: IAM ensures that only authorized users have access to network resources. By controlling access to the resources, organizations can restrict the access rights of individuals based on their job function, location, and other factors.

2.   Regulatory Compliance: Organizations must comply with various regulatory requirements, such as GDPR and HIPAA. IAM solutions enable organizations to maintain compliance and manage access to sensitive data by using policies that align with these regulations.

3.   Increased productivity: IAM solutions can boost productivity by simplifying user access to network resources. This includes the use of single sign-on (SSO) and multi-factor authentication (MFA), which prevent users from having to remember multiple passwords for different applications and systems.

4.   Enhanced Security: IAM solutions provide an extra layer of protection against cyber-attacks by ensuring that only authorized individuals can access network resources. By preventing unauthorized access, these solutions boost the security posture of organizations.

In summary, IAM is an essential component of an organization's security strategy. It helps organizations to manage and control access to network resources, ensures regulatory compliance, boosts productivity, and enhances security against cyberattacks. By implementing IAM solutions, organizations can improve their security posture and protect their digital assets from potential threats.

4.15   Can you discuss the importance of red teaming and blue teaming exercises in cybersecurity?

Red teaming and blue teaming are two complementary methodologies in cybersecurity that help organizations proactively assess and improve their defenses. Red teaming exercises involve a simulated attack scenario where a team of skilled hackers tries to breach an organization's security controls and gain access to sensitive data or systems. On the other hand, blue teaming exercises involve a team of internal security professionals who defend against the simulated attacks and work to identify and mitigate security vulnerabilities.

Here are some reasons why red teaming and blue teaming exercises are important in cybersecurity:

1. Assessing security posture: Red teaming exercises provide insights on the effectiveness of current security controls and the vulnerability of an organization's network and infrastructure. Such an assessment can help an organization identify gaps in its defenses, including software vulnerabilities, gaps in security policies or procedures, and weaknesses in system configurations.

2. Training and education: Red teaming exercises provide a training opportunity for the blue team, who can learn from observing the attackers and responding to various attack scenarios. This exercise also helps to educate both teams on the latest tactics, techniques, and procedures used by threat actors, and can aid in creating more effective security procedures.

3. Strengthening risk management: Identifying vulnerabilities can help organizations prioritize which risks are most significant

and where resources should be allocated to mitigate the risks.

4. Preparing for incidents: Red teaming exercises simulate real-world attacks, making the blue team better prepared for a real attack. This exercise provides an opportunity to review incident response plans and identify any gaps that need to be addressed.

5. Providing compliance: Red team/blue team exercises are becoming increasingly important to demonstrate to regulators that a company is effectively implementing reasonable security measures. This can help organizations meet compliance requirements and demonstrate to customers that their data is being protected.

In summary, red teaming and blue teaming exercises are essential in cybersecurity to identify vulnerabilities, educate teams, prioritize risk, and prepare organizations for incident response. By proactively assessing and strengthening defenses against threats, organizations can prevent security breaches, protect valuable data, and preserve their reputation.

4.16 What is the role of cyber threat hunting in a proactive cybersecurity approach?

Cyber threat hunting is a proactive approach to identify and detect potential cyber threats that may have gone unnoticed by traditional security measures such as firewalls or antivirus software. It involves actively searching for signs of suspicious activity or behavior in an organization's network or endpoints.

In a proactive cybersecurity approach, cyber threat hunting plays a critical role in identifying and mitigating potential security incidents before they turn into a full-blown attack. By continuously proactively searching for vulnerabilities in the network, organizations can identify security gaps that may not be addressed by traditional security measures.

One of the key benefits of cyber threat hunting is that it helps to reduce the time between when a breach occurs and when it is detected. This is critical because attackers can move quickly to exfiltrate data or cause damage once they have infiltrated an organization's network. By quickly identifying and mitigating potential threats, organizations can minimize the damage caused by an attack.

Cyber threat hunting can also help organizations identify threats that may be targeting specific vulnerabilities or weaknesses in their systems or infrastructure. For example, if an organization is using an older version of an operating system or a vulnerable software application, cyber threat hunting can help identify potential threats that are targeting these specific vulnerabilities.

In summary, cyber threat hunting is an important proactive approach in cybersecurity. It helps organizations to identify and mitigate potential threats before they can cause significant damage to the network or infrastructure. By continuously monitoring for signs of suspicious activity, organizations can improve their overall security posture and reduce the risk of a successful cyber attack.

4.17   What is a supply chain attack, and how can organizations protect themselves from such attacks?

A supply chain attack is a type of cyber attack that targets the systems and networks of a third-party supplier, vendor, or service provider to gain unauthorized access or manipulate their products, software, or hardware, with the aim of compromising the security or integrity of the end-users who rely on these components. The goal of a supply chain attack is to exploit the trust between the supplier and their customers to launch a successful attack.

One common example of a supply chain attack is a software poisoning attack. In this scenario, an attacker can insert rogue code or malware into a legitimate software update or application library used by a third-party vendor or supplier. When customers download the update or the library, the malicious code is installed alongside the legitimate code, giving the attacker a foothold into the customers' networks and data.

Another example of a supply chain attack is hardware tampering. This involves an attacker physically modifying a product or component during the manufacturing or shipping process, such as adding a malicious component or opening a backdoor implant in a router or mobile device. When the product is eventually deployed, the attacker can use these vulnerabilities to gain access and control over the end-user's systems.

To protect themselves against supply chain attacks, organizations can take several steps, including:

1. Risk assessment: Conducting a thorough risk assessment

of the suppliers and vendors in their supply chain to identify potential vulnerabilities and assess their trustworthiness.

2. Vendor management: Establishing clear policies and procedures for vendor management, including due diligence, contract management, and ongoing monitoring to detect any suspicious activity or deviations from the agreed-upon security standards.

3. Security testing: Conducting regular security testing and vulnerability assessments of the applications, software, and hardware components used in the organization's supply chain to identify and remediate any security loopholes and weaknesses.

4. Security controls: Implementing strong security controls and best practices, such as multi-factor authentication, encryption, and access controls, to enforce the principle of least privilege and limit the exposure of sensitive data and critical systems.

5. Incident response: Establishing a robust incident response plan that outlines the steps to be taken in the event of a supply chain attack, including communication, containment, and recovery.

Overall, proactive risk management and ongoing monitoring are essential to detecting and mitigating supply chain attacks before they can cause significant damage to an organization's data, networks, and reputation.

4.18 How do you ensure the security of APIs in a microservices architecture?

In a microservices architecture, APIs serve as the primary communication mechanism between different microservices. Therefore, securing APIs is critical to ensuring the overall security of the microservices architecture. Here are some ways to ensure the security of APIs in a microservices architecture:

1. Use Authentication and Authorization: APIs should be secured with proper authentication and authorization mechanisms. Authentication ensures that only authorized users can access the APIs, while authorization ensures that users can only access the APIs that they are authorized to access. The use of OAuth and OpenID Connect are popular authentication mechanisms for REST APIs.

2. Implement HTTPS: HTTPS should be used to secure the communication between the client and server. It ensures that the data is encrypted in transit and prevents eavesdropping, tampering, and other forms of attacks.

3. Use API Gateway: An API Gateway acts as a single entry point for all the APIs in the microservices architecture. It can perform functions such as authentication, authorization, rate limiting, and traffic shaping, ensuring that only the intended traffic reaches the microservices.

4. Monitor APIs: Regular monitoring of APIs is necessary to identify potential security threats and take appropriate actions to mitigate them. Monitoring can include tracking API usage, collecting metrics, logging, and alerting.

5. Implement Rate Limiting: Rate limiting is a mechanism that ensures that an API can only be used within predefined limits. This can include the number of requests per second or per minute. Rate limiting prevents brute force attacks and helps preserve server resources.

6. Implement Input Validation: Input validation ensures that only expected data is accepted by APIs. This can prevent common attacks such as SQL injection and cross-site scripting.

7. Use a Web Application Firewall (WAF): A WAF is designed to protect web applications against common attacks, such as SQL injection and cross-site scripting. It helps to check the incoming requests against known attack signatures and block them if identified.

In summary, securing APIs in a microservices architecture requires the implementation of multiple security controls. By adopting these recommended practices, you will help ensure the overall security and integrity of your microservices architecture.

4.19 What is the concept of just-in-time (JIT) access, and how can it be applied to enhance security in an organization?

Just-in-time access (JIT) is a privilege management approach that allows users to access resources or applications only when they are needed, for a specific period of time. JIT access is meant to reduce the attack surface by limiting a user's access to only those resources that they require, and for the duration they need them. JIT access is becoming a popular security practice in many organizations, especially those that prioritize a defense-in-depth cybersecurity strategy.

When applied, JIT access enables an organization to enhance security and to prevent unauthorized access to critical systems or files. With JIT access, organizations can quickly remove the access rights of a user once they have completed a task, or when the access rights are no longer required. This reduces the risk of unauthorized access and helps to prevent privilege escalation attacks.

The following are some ways that JIT access enhances security in organizations:

1. Reduces the Attack Surface: JIT access reduces the attack surface by limiting a user's access to only those resources that they require, and only during the duration they need them. This kind of access greatly reduces the risk of an attacker gaining access to a system or resource that they shouldn't have access to.

2. Stronger Access Controls: The JIT process provides stronger access controls, as users can only access resources or applications when they need them. Additionally, it is easier for the IT team to monitor and track user access to resources, applications or system components.

3. Prevents Insider Threats: JIT access can prevent insider attacks by limiting a user's access to only the necessary resources. This means that even if an authorized user decides to abuse their privilege, the impact is significantly reduced.

4. Mitigates the Impact of External Attacks: If an external

attacker succeeds in penetrating an organization's security defenses, JIT access can limit the extent of the breach. With access to only specific systems or applications, an attacker would find it difficult to move laterally across the network and access sensitive information.

5. Ensures Compliance: JIT access can help organizations adhere to industry regulations and security standards by ensuring that users only access the resources that they are authorized to access for a specific period of time.

To implement JIT access, an organization needs to have a robust Identity and Access Management (IAM) framework in place. IAM should include different components such as authentication, authorization, and monitoring. IAM solutions such as Microsoft Azure AD provide just-in-time access that allows temporary access to resources, enabling secure access without creating permanent access pathways.

In conclusion, JIT access is a cybersecurity approach that secures an organization's systems, resources and data by providing users with the exact access they need for a specific period of time. By implementing JIT access, an organization enhances its cybersecurity posture, minimizing the risks of data breaches, insider attacks, and unauthorized access to critical resources.

4.20 Can you explain the role of security awareness training in reducing the risk of human error in cybersecurity incidents?

The majority of cybersecurity incidents are caused by human errors such as clicking on a malicious link, falling for a phishing scam, weak passwords, or failing to update software. Human errors are one of the greatest causes of cybersecurity breaches, which may cause a lot of harm to an organization, such as loss of data, financial loss, reputational damage, and legal liability.

Therefore, cybersecurity awareness training plays a vital role in reducing the risk of human error in cybersecurity incidents. Here are some ways that security awareness training can help:

1. Educating Employees: Security awareness training helps to educate employees on how they can protect themselves and the organization from cyber threats. They will learn how to identify potential cybersecurity risks and what steps they can take to avoid them. Through training, they will understand the importance of maintaining secure passwords, avoiding phishing scams, and suspicious attachments.

2. Mitigating Phishing Attacks: One of the most significant risks to organizations is the human susceptibility to phishing attacks. Effective security awareness training can teach employees to identify suspicious emails, avoid clicking on malicious links, and not share sensitive information through email or social media.

3. Improving Password Security: Passwords are one of the most

straightforward ways for cybercriminals to access an organization's network. Security awareness training can teach employees about password best practices such as using complex and unique passwords, not sharing passwords, and not reusing passwords across multiple accounts.

4. Proper Device Use: Employees need to understand how to use their devices correctly, whether they are using work computers or mobile devices. Security awareness training can teach employees about the dangers of downloading software and apps from untrusted sources, and how to keep their devices updated with the latest patches and security updates.

In conclusion, security awareness training is an essential component of any cybersecurity program. By educating employees on cybersecurity best practices, organizations can reduce the risk of human error and improve their overall cybersecurity posture.

Chapter 5

Expert

5.1 How do you approach developing a cybersecurity strategy for an organization?

The development of a cybersecurity strategy for an organization is a complex process that requires a thorough understanding of the organization's business objectives, risk tolerance, and threat landscape. Here are some steps to approach this process:

1. Identify and assess risks: The first step is to identify and assess the risks associated with the organization's data, systems, and network. This can be done by conducting a comprehensive risk assessment that identifies potential threats, vulnerabilities, and impacts. This may include analyzing past security incidents or attacks, conducting penetration testing, and reviewing policies and procedures.

2. Define cybersecurity objectives: Once the risks are identified, the next step is to define the cybersecurity objectives for the organization. This involves identifying the assets that need protection and determining the level of protection required. The objectives should be aligned with the business objectives and reflect the organization's risk tolerance.

3. Develop a cybersecurity policy: A cybersecurity policy outlines the organization's expectations for employees, vendors, and partners regarding cybersecurity. It should establish rules and guidelines for accessing and using the organization's network, systems, and data. It should also define the roles and responsibilities for managing cybersecurity risks and incidents.

4. Establish a security architecture: A security architecture is a framework that outlines the technology, processes, and controls required to protect the organization's data and systems. It should be designed to prevent, detect, and respond to security incidents. This may include firewalls, intrusion detection systems, encryption, and access controls.

5. Implement cybersecurity controls: Once the objectives, policy, and architecture are in place, the next step is to implement cybersecurity controls. This involves deploying technology, processes, and procedures to protect the organization's data and systems. This may include installing security software, monitoring systems, and implementing security awareness training for employees.

6. Monitor and evaluate: The final step is to monitor and evaluate the effectiveness of the cybersecurity strategy. This involves reviewing security logs, conducting regular risk assessments, and testing the security architecture. The strategy should be updated regularly to reflect changes in the threat landscape and

business environment.

Overall, the development of a cybersecurity strategy for an organization is a continuous process that requires ongoing monitoring and evaluation. It requires collaboration between IT, security, and business stakeholders to ensure that the organization's data and systems are adequately protected.

5.2 Can you discuss some methods for measuring the effectiveness of a cybersecurity program?

Measuring the effectiveness of a cybersecurity program can be a complex task as there are multiple factors that need to be taken into account. However, the following methods can be used to measure the effectiveness of a cybersecurity program:

1. Risk assessments: Conducting risk assessments can help identify vulnerabilities and potential threats that an organization may face. Risk assessments also help the organization to prioritize security controls and evaluate the impact of controls on reducing risks.

2. Compliance audits: Compliance audits help in determining whether the organization's cybersecurity program is aligned with applicable laws, regulations, and standards such as HIPAA, PCI-DSS, NIST, etc. An organization can also perform self-assessments to maintain compliance.

3. Penetration testing: Penetration testing involves attempting to exploit vulnerabilities in an organization's systems and net-

work to see how easily a hacker can gain unauthorized access. It helps in identifying weaknesses and testing the effectiveness of security controls.

4. Security incidents and response management: Analyzing incidents of cyberattacks and how they were handled can help measure the effectiveness of the cybersecurity program. This includes detecting incidents, responding to them, mitigating their impacts, and recovering from them.

5. Employee security awareness: Educating employees on cybersecurity best practices and monitoring their adherence to security policies can help measure the effectiveness of the program. Organizations can conduct phishing simulations and other forms of training to evaluate employee awareness.

6. Continuous monitoring: Regularly monitoring the network, endpoints, and applications can help detect potential security threats and anomalies. This can include security information and event management (SIEM), intrusion detection systems (IDS), and other forms of monitoring.

Overall, measuring the effectiveness of a cybersecurity program involves a combination of assessing risks, compliance, testing security controls, managing security incidents, educating employees, and continuous monitoring. By using these methods, an organization can gain insights into the effectiveness of its cybersecurity program and make necessary adjustments to improve it.

5.3 What are the main challenges in securing a hybrid cloud environment, and how can they be addressed?

Hybrid cloud environments, which comprise a combination of public, private, and on-premise infrastructure, pose unique security challenges due to their complexity, heterogeneity, and distributed nature. Below are some of the main challenges that organizations may face when securing a hybrid cloud environment, as well as some potential solutions:

1. Data protection: One of the biggest concerns in a hybrid cloud environment is ensuring that sensitive data is adequately protected, whether it is stored in the cloud or being transferred between different environments. Encryption is a crucial tool for data protection, as it can secure data at rest and in transit against unauthorized access. Additionally, access controls, role-based permissions, and network segmentation can help limit access to sensitive data to authorized users and systems.

2. Visibility and control: Another challenge in a hybrid cloud environment is maintaining visibility and control over all the different components, applications, and workloads. This requires comprehensive monitoring and governance tools that can provide real-time insights into the entire hybrid landscape, as well as the ability to manage and enforce policies across all environments. Cloud access security brokers (CASBs) can also help organizations gain visibility and control over cloud services by providing access controls, threat protection, and data loss prevention.

3. Identity and access management: With multiple environments, it can be difficult to ensure that users and systems have

the appropriate level of access and authentication. Managing identity and access across hybrid environments requires a centralized identity and access management (IAM) solution that can provide single sign-on (SSO), multi-factor authentication (MFA), and role-based access control (RBAC). IAM solutions can also help enforce security policies and compliance regulations across all environments.

4. Integration and automation: Integrating different systems, applications, and tools across hybrid environments is another challenge that can introduce security risks if not done properly. Automation can help simplify the integration process and reduce the risk of human error, while also providing consistency and scalability. DevSecOps practices can also help promote security and quality at every stage of the software development lifecycle by integrating security testing and feedback into the development process.

5. Compliance and governance: Compliance and governance are critical for organizations to maintain regulatory compliance and meet audit requirements, especially in highly regulated industries. Hybrid cloud environments require a unified governance framework that can provide clear policies and procedures for all environments. Tools such as infrastructure as code (IaC), configuration management, and vulnerability management can help ensure that all environments are compliant, secure, and up-to-date with the latest security and compliance standards.

In summary, securing a hybrid cloud environment requires a multifaceted approach that addresses the unique challenges posed by the distributed, heterogeneous environment. Strong data protection practices, enhanced visibility and control, robust identity and access management, automation, and compliance and governance frameworks are all essential components of an effective hybrid cloud security strategy.

5.4 What are some advanced techniques for detecting and preventing lateral movement within a network?

Lateral movement within a network is a critical part of a cyber attacker's strategy to compromise endpoints and expand their reach within the network. Therefore, detecting and preventing lateral movement is critical to reducing the impact of a cyber-attack. Let's discuss some advanced techniques to detect and prevent lateral movement within a network:

1. Network Segmentation: Network segmentation is the process of dividing a network into smaller subnetworks. This technique isolates critical systems and reduces the impact of a security breach. It's hard for attackers to move laterally within segmented networks, as the movement is limited.

2. Network Traffic Analysis: Network traffic analysis is a technique that involves monitoring network traffic for suspicious activity. It detects and alerts security teams of any unusual network behavior that could be associated with lateral movement. For instance, if an attacker is trying to access sensitive data or make unauthorized connections, network traffic analysis can detect and block the activity.

3. Endpoint Detection and Response (EDR): EDR is a security solution that involves monitoring and response capabilities. This technique identifies and responds to suspicious activity within the endpoint network. It detects the attacker's attempts

to move laterally within the network, blocks them, and informs security teams.

4. Privileged Account Management (PAM): PAM helps control privileged access to resources within a network. PAM works by monitoring and controlling access to privileged accounts to reduce the possibility of lateral movement. In the case of a breach, PAM provides an audit trail of activities, which helps determine the scope of the attack.

5. User Behavior Analytics (UBA): UBA is a technique that involves monitoring user behavior to identify unusual and potentially malicious activity. It detects when the attacker uses a compromised account to move laterally through the network, making it easier to stop the attacker's progression through the network.

6. Deception Technology: Deception technology deceives attackers by presenting fake systems or data to tempt them to enter the environment. Deception technology lures attackers into engaging with decoys, which helps security teams detect and prevent lateral movement.

In summary, it's essential to implement multiple layers of protection to detect and prevent lateral movement within a network. Advanced techniques like network segmentation, network traffic analysis, EDR, PAM, UBA, and deception technology can all help with this. No technique alone can provide complete security; it's a combination of these techniques that's crucial to protect your network.

5.5 How do you approach securing a large-scale distributed system, such as a big data environment or a high-performance computing cluster?

Securing a large-scale distributed system, such as a big data environment or a high-performance computing cluster, involves addressing several security challenges. The following is an approach for securing such systems:

1. Conduct a risk assessment: A comprehensive risk assessment is essential to identify potential security risks and vulnerabilities. This assessment should cover both external and internal threats, such as malware attacks, denial-of-service attacks, insider threats, and data breaches.

2. Develop a security plan: Based on the findings of the risk assessment, develop a security plan tailored to the specific needs and requirements of the distributed system. The plan should address areas such as access control, network security, data protection, and incident response.

3. Apply security controls: Apply security controls to the distributed system to mitigate security risks. These controls can include firewalls, intrusion detection systems, data encryption, and virtual private networks (VPNs). Access controls should be implemented to ensure only authorized personnel have access to resources within the system.

4. Monitor the system: Implement a security monitoring system to detect any suspicious activity on the system. This monitoring system should include real-time analysis of log data,

network traffic, and system activity. The system should also provide alerts to security staff when any security events are detected.

5. Perform regular audits: Regular audits of the distributed system should be conducted to ensure that security controls are being enforced and that the system is compliant with relevant security and regulatory standards. Regular auditing can also help identify any new security risks and vulnerabilities that need to be addressed.

Examples of security challenges in distributed systems include:

- Data breaches: Large-scale distributed systems often store a significant amount of sensitive data. Any data breaches can have severe consequences, such as reputational damage, financial loss, and legal penalties.

- Insider threats: Deploying large-scale distributed systems means granting access to many users, which increases the risk of insider threats. Malicious insiders can cause significant damage if they gain access to the system's data or resources.

- Network security: Distributed systems are vulnerable to network attacks, such as man-in-the-middle attacks or distributed denial-of-service (DDoS) attacks. To address this challenge, network security measures such as encryption, firewalls, and intrusion detection systems can be deployed.

- Software vulnerabilities: Distributed systems often run complex software stacks that may contain security vulnerabilities. These vulnerabilities can be exploited by attackers to gain unauthorized access to the system.

In summary, securing large-scale distributed systems requires a holistic approach. This approach must be tailored to the specific needs and requirements of the system, including network security, access control, data protection, and incident response. Regular audits and monitoring are essential to ensure that the system's security controls are effective, and risks are mitigated.

5.6 What are some common issues in managing third-party risk, and how can they be mitigated?

Managing third-party risk can be a complex task with various challenges. Some of the common issues faced in managing third-party risks are:

1. Lack of visibility: Due to the limited visibility into a third-party's operations, products or services, it becomes difficult to assess their risk posture accurately.

2. Compliance challenges: The third-party may not be compliant with regulatory requirements, which can lead to reputational, legal, or financial risk for the organization.

3. Data breaches: Third-party vendors may have inadequate security controls, which increase the risk of data breaches, and loss of sensitive information.

4. Lack of trust: Trust between the organization and its third-party vendor can be strained if the vendor fails to deliver on promises.

To mitigate these risks, companies can adopt the following measures:

1. Conduct thorough risk assessments: Conducting due diligence to assess the third-party's security posture, compliance status, and reputation can help identify potential risks.

2. Implement effective contracts: Contracts should stipulate compliance with regulations and can include clauses that hold third-party vendors accountable for any breaches.

3. Implement monitoring and oversight mechanisms: Establishing controls for detecting and reporting unusual activity can reduce the risk of data breaches, and regular monitoring can help avoid potential issues.

4. Invest in cybersecurity measures: Third-party vendors should be required to have adequate cybersecurity measures in place, such as firewalls, encryption, and multi-factor authentication.

5. Build a strong relationship: Building a good relationship with the vendor can enhance transparency, trust, and responsiveness, reducing the risk of potential problems.

In conclusion, managing third-party risk requires a comprehensive and continuous approach, and effective communication between the organization and its vendors. Organizations need to identify the risks and put in place measures to overcome them for a successful relationship with third-party vendors, earning mutual trust and confidence.

5.7 How do you approach integrating security into the DevOps process (i.e., DevSecOps)?

Integrating security into the DevOps process to create "DevSec-Ops" is becoming increasingly important due to the growing number of cyber attacks and the need to deploy software faster in a continuous manner.

Here are six steps to consider for integrating security into the DevOps process:

1. Educate the Teams: Begin educating everyone involved in the DevSecOps process, including developers, operations personnel, security teams, and testers, about their roles and responsibilities for security. This includes topics such as secure coding practices, vulnerability management, penetration testing, and more.

2. Shift Left: Shift security to earlier in the development process, rather than waiting until the code is in testing or production. Always consider security as an integral part of the development process from the outset. By using tools such as static code analysis, security testing, and threat modeling in the earliest stages, vulnerabilities can be detected and remediated before deployment.

3. Automate Security Testing: Automated testing tools are necessary to enable continuous deployment in DevSecOps. These tools can identify vulnerabilities in real-time, automatically generate threat reports, and integrate with other tools used in the DevSecOps pipeline.

4. Monitor for Threats: Continuous monitoring for threats is a key aspect of DevSecOps. Use automated tools that can monitor for vulnerabilities and suspicious activity, and then alert operations or security teams to respond to potential threats.

5. Implement a Security Culture: Create a culture of security awareness that is embedded in DevSecOps practices. Encourage all team members to report suspicious behavior or potential threats as soon as possible.

6. Perform Audits and Penetration Testing: Regular audits and penetration testing can help identify security weaknesses in the DevSecOps process. By performing regular security assessments, the teams can take proactive steps to remediate vulnerabilities and strengthen the security posture of their systems.

For instance, let's say that there is a DevOps team focused on creating a mobile application that will allow users to transfer money easily between accounts. To ensure security is integrated from the beginning, the team could send developers for training to understand secure coding practices, use automated testing tools to continually monitor for vulnerabilities, and perform periodic penetration testing to identify potential vulnerabilities. The team would also put precautions in place and have a plan in case of cyber attacks or their database is stolen. With these measures in place, the team would have a strong DevSecOps process in place that would help ensure the application is secure from start to finish.

5.8 Can you discuss the concept of continuous security monitoring and its importance in maintaining a strong security posture?

Continuous Security Monitoring (CSM) is the practice of dynamically and actively monitoring an organization's entire IT environment on an ongoing basis to identify security risks and vulnerabilities. It is important to maintain a strong security posture because it provides real-time visibility into potential security issues, helps organizations quickly detect anomalies, and responds effectively to incidents, minimizing the impact of a potential security breach.

One important aspect of CSM is the use of advanced toolsets that detect data breaches and attacks in real-time. CSM toolsets provide the capability to quickly detect signs of compromise or malicious activity that may be a precursor to a full-scale attack. Examples of such tools include Security Information and Event Management (SIEM) systems, which monitor network traffic patterns, analyze logs from various sources, and provide alerts on potential malicious behavior.

Another important aspect of CSM is monitoring user activity. This includes monitoring system usage and analyzing user behavior to identify any insider threats, such as employees with access to sensitive data attempting to steal or exfiltrate such data. User activity monitoring also helps organizations to quickly identify unauthorized access, which in turn can help reduce the time to detect and respond to a security incident.

A well-designed CSM program should also include regular vulnerability assessments and testing to identify and address any gaps in security controls. This can be achieved using tools and methodologies such as penetration testing, vulnerability scanning, and red teaming.

In conclusion, continuous security monitoring is an essential component of any modern cybersecurity program. By providing real-time visibility into potential threats and vulnerabilities, organizations can proactively take steps to mitigate risks and prevent security incidents. It allows security teams to make informed decisions based on accurate and up-to-date information and helps them move toward maintaining a proactive security posture.

5.9   What is the role of a security architect in an organization, and what are some key considerations in designing secure systems?

A security architect is responsible for designing and implementing secure systems in an organization. The primary role of a security architect is to assess the security risks of an organization and develop plans to mitigate those risks using appropriate security technologies, processes, and policies.

Key considerations in designing secure systems include understanding the threat landscape, designing the system with security in mind, and implementing security controls to protect against potential threats.

Understanding the threat landscape requires identifying potential attackers and the methods they might use to compromise the system. For instance, a security architect designing a system for a financial institution must consider the potential for phishing attacks, malware, insider threats, and other risks.

Designing the system with security in mind involves using secure architectures, programming languages, and development processes that can help mitigate security risks. Security architects must also consider data protection, application security, network security, and other key security areas when designing a system.

Implementing security controls involves designing security policies and procedures that govern the use of the system, including access control, auditing, monitoring, and incident response. Security architects must also implement technical security controls, such as firewalls, intrusion detection and prevention systems, and encryption mechanisms.

Overall, the role of a security architect is critical to maintaining the security of an organization's information assets. By designing and implementing secure systems, security architects help to protect organizations from cyber attacks, data breaches, and other security incidents.

5.10 How do you approach balancing security and usability when designing and implementing security controls?

Balancing security and usability is an essential part of cybersecurity. Security controls are designed to protect an organization's assets from unauthorized access or theft, but those controls can also hinder usability for legitimate users. Therefore, it is essential to establish a balance between security and usability.

Here are some practical approaches that can be taken to balance security and usability:

1. Risk Assessment: Conduct thorough risk assessments to determine what security controls are necessary to protect your organization's assets adequately. It helps to identify potential risks and vulnerabilities, so you can design effective security controls to combat them.

2. User Experience Testing: Before implementing security controls, always perform user testing. It helps to ensure that the security measures you create do not impact usability negatively. User experience testing can reveal how users will be affected by the security measures that have been put in place. Based on this feedback, you may be able to modify the security controls or put in place alternative measures that will minimize the negative impact on usability without compromising security.

3. Educate Users: A critical component of balancing security and usability is user education. Educating your users on the importance of security controls creates awareness and helps users appreciate the significance of the measures that have been introduced. They are more likely to comply with security rules when they understand the rationale behind them.

4. Propose Alternatives Solutions: In situations where security controls are deemed non-negotiable, suggest alternative solutions, such as Single Sign-On (SSO) or Multi-Factor Authentication (MFA) to improve usability. SSO and MFA can serve as practical solutions that still maintain a high level of security

without becoming too cumbersome for users.

5. Regular Review: Undertake regular reviews of your security measures to ensure that they remain effective and continue to balance security with usability. As the threat landscape changes, so will your organization's risk profile, and the effectiveness of the security measures you have put in place. Therefore, it is essential to conduct regular evaluations to ensure that they are still one step ahead of any evolving threats.

To sum up, striking the balance between usability and security is critical. By conducting risk assessments, training your users, and regularly evaluating your security measures' effectiveness, you can create a robust security posture without losing sight of usability.

5.11 What are the main challenges in securing mobile devices and applications, and how can they be addressed?

Mobile devices and applications have become an integral part of our daily lives. However, their wide usage and portability create significant security concerns. Here are some of the main security challenges in securing mobile devices and applications and how to address them:

1. Device Fragmentation: There are multiple operating systems, versions, and device types in the mobile ecosystem. Software updates, security patches, and policy enforcement become a significant challenge due to the diversity of devices.

Solution: Mobile device management (MDM) and enterprise mobility management (EMM) solutions can help enterprises manage and secure devices, applications and data on all types of mobile devices.

2. Data Leakage: Mobile devices often contain sensitive corporate data that can be compromised when lost, stolen, or hacked.

Solution: Encryption of data at rest and in transit helps safeguard confidential information from unauthorized access or disclosure. The use of biometric (e.g., fingerprint or facial recognition) authentication or multi-factor authentication, such as verifying a users identity through their mobile phones, also enhances mobile device security.

3. Malicious Apps: Cybercriminals leverage popular application repositories like Google Play Store or Apple App Store to distribute malicious apps that can steal sensitive data or compromise the device.

Solution: The use of mobile threat defense (MTD) software, along with regular security audits and testing of applications, can help identify and remediate potential security loopholes or vulnerabilities.

4. Insider Threats: Insiders with authorized access to mobile devices can intentionally or unintentionally compromise confidential data.

Solution: Establishing governance policies, employee training, and background checks can help mitigate insider threats. Also, regular auditing of device usage and alerting mechanisms can detect and prevent potential threats.

5. Social Engineering: Social engineering attacks on mobile de-

vices can deceive users to reveal sensitive information or download malware.

Solution: Security awareness and education programs can help employees recognize and avoid such attacks. Also, the use of anti-virus or anti-malware tools can help detect and block malicious software

In conclusion, safeguarding mobile devices and their associated applications is vital for businesses and individuals. Enterprises must establish comprehensive security policies, deploy security technologies and software, and conduct regular security audits to stay ahead of potential threats. End-to-end security is important to ensure that data is protected from the device level to the network level, and personnel training is also crucial.

5.12 Can you discuss the importance of cyber resilience and its relationship to traditional cybersecurity efforts?

Cyber resilience is the ability to prepare for, respond to, and recover from a cyber attack or incident. It involves a proactive and holistic approach to cybersecurity that focuses not only on preventing breaches but also on being able to quickly detect and respond to them, minimize damage, and maintain business continuity. In other words, it's about building a strong cybersecurity posture that is prepared for and can withstand cyber threats.

In today's fast-paced and interconnected digital landscape, traditional cybersecurity measures such as firewalls, antivirus software, and encryption are no longer sufficient to protect against sophisticated and evolving cyber threats. Cyber resilience incorporates a range of practices, technologies, and processes that complement traditional cybersecurity efforts and create a more comprehensive and effective defense.

Here are some examples of how cyber resilience can enhance traditional cybersecurity measures:

1. Risk assessment and management: Cyber resilience involves conducting regular risk assessments to identify vulnerabilities and potential threats to an organization's IT systems and data. By identifying and prioritizing risks, organizations can better allocate resources and prioritize cybersecurity efforts to address the most critical vulnerabilities.

2. Incident response planning: Having a well-structured and tested incident response plan is a critical component of cyber resilience. Such a plan should include procedures for detecting, analyzing, containing, and remediating cybersecurity incidents quickly and effectively to minimize damage and downtime.

3. Business continuity planning: Cyber resilience also requires developing and testing business continuity plans to ensure that critical systems and operations can continue operating in the event of a cyber attack or other disruptive event.

4. Training and awareness: Cyber resilience involves educating employees on identifying and responding to cyber threats, such as phishing attacks, social engineering, and other malware. This can help prevent incidents before they occur and also help employees detect and report incidents more quickly.

Overall, cyber resilience is a proactive approach to cybersecurity that recognizes the inevitability of cyber attacks and focuses on being prepared to respond quickly, minimize damage, and maintain business continuity. By enhancing traditional cybersecurity measures with these practices, organizations can create a strong and robust defense against cyber threats.

5.13 How do you approach creating a culture of security within an organization?

Creating a culture of security within an organization involves a series of steps that must be taken intentionally to promote secure practices and integrate security into every aspect of an organization's operations. Here are some ways to approach creating a culture of security within an organization:

1. Develop a security policy: First and foremost, a security policy that outlines the organization's security measures, protocols, and best practices must be developed. The policy should also address the roles and responsibilities of employees with respect to security.

2. Educate employees about cyber threats: The employees must be educated about the various types of cyber threats such as phishing, malware, ransomware, social engineering, etc. They should also be informed about the best practices to avoid these threats, such as strong password creation, identifying malicious emails or links, and so on.

3. Encourage employee participation: Encouraging employee participation is a crucial step in creating a culture of security.

Whether its an internal competition or workshops, involving employees in security initiatives can make a big difference. Employees must know that they are valued members of the organization's security force, and their contribution is valuable in protecting the organization from cyber threats.

4. Regularly conduct security awareness training: Security awareness training sessions should be conducted at regular intervals to reinforce employees understanding of security measures and the importance of following them.

5. Implement a reward system: Establishing a reward system for employees who demonstrate good security practices can create a positive reinforcement system. This can encourage employees to be more diligent when practicing security measures.

6. Conduct regular security audits: Regular security audits must be conducted to ensure compliance with security policies and to identify vulnerabilities. Conducting these security audits can assure employees that security is a top priority and create a sense of accountability.

7. Have a contingency plan in place: Its important to have a contingency plan in place in case of a security incident. Employees should be trained on the steps to take in case of a security breach or other incident.

In summary, creating a culture of security within an organization is a step-by-step process that should begin with a security policy and evolve into regular training, audits, and employee participation. Through such efforts, the organization can establish a culture where employees prioritize security in every aspect of their work, reducing the risks of cyber threats.

5.14 What are some key considerations in designing and implementing a secure remote work environment?

With the rise of remote work, ensuring a secure remote work environment has become a critical aspect of business operations. Here are some key considerations in designing and implementing a secure remote work environment:

1. Establish strong authentication protocols: Remote workers should be required to authenticate their identity through strong authentication protocols such as multifactor authentication (MFA), biometrics, or smart cards before accessing sensitive data or applications. Implementing MFA reduces the chances of unauthorized access to sensitive data even when authentication credentials have been compromised.

2. Secure remote access: Remote access to the company's network should be facilitated through a secure VPN connection. This helps to encrypt all communication between the remote worker's device and the company network. Tight security measures, such as firewalls and intrusion detection systems, should also be in place to prevent unauthorized access to the network.

3. Secure communication: Encrypted communication channels should be used for all remote communications to prevent eavesdropping or interception of sensitive information. Encrypted email, messaging services, and video conference calls must be used when communicating sensitive information.

4. Secure Devices: All remote work devices must be secured with up-to-date antimalware and antivirus software solutions. Personal devices should not be used for work-related tasks, es-

pecially when dealing with sensitive data such as financial data or intellectual property.

5. Regular updates and patching: Regularly applying software updates and patches is key to keeping remote devices secure. Employees must be educated on the importance of regularly applying software updates, and compliance must be enforced.

6. Strong Passwords: Employees must be required to use strong passwords and avoid using the same password for multiple accounts. Using Password Managers can help users store and create complex passwords. Passwords should also be changed on a regular basis.

7. Data Backup: To prevent data loss, all remote workers should be required to backup their work regularly. Additionally, cloud backup services should be used to ensure that all work-related data is backed up and recoverable in the event of a disaster or data breach.

By addressing each of these key considerations when designing and implementing a remote work environment, organizations can provide a secure remote work environment that protects sensitive data and intellectual property from potential cyber threats.

5.15 How do you approach the process of securing and managing the lifecycle of cryptographic keys?

The process of securing and managing cryptographic keys is vital for maintaining data confidentiality, integrity, and authenticity. The following are some essential steps for securing and managing cryptographic keys throughout their lifecycle:

1) Key Creation: First, a secure and trusted cryptographic algorithm should be selected for generating the keys. Once the keys are generated, they should be kept in an encrypted and secure environment.

2) Key Distribution: Keys should only be distributed to authorized personnel with the necessary privileges. The most widely used method for distribution is by exchanging keys over a secure network encrypted with symmetric encryption algorithms such as AES or by using asymmetric encryption like RSA.

3) Key Storage: Cryptographic keys should be stored securely and protected by a security mechanism like a Hardware Security Module (HSM). These devices provide tamper-proof protection for cryptographic keys and ensure secure storage.

4) Key Usage: Cryptographic keys should be used as per the organization's security protocols and policies, using cryptographic protocols validated by standards organizations like NIST (National Institute of Standards and Technology).

5) Key Maintenance: Maintenance of cryptographic keys involves regularly backing up keys, updating and patching key management systems, controlling access, and regular key rota-

tion to prevent key compromise.

6) Key Termination: When cryptographic keys are no longer needed, they should be destroyed securely. This can be achieved by systematically purging them from the system and then securely deleting them.

In summary, securing and managing cryptographic keys is a vital process for maintaining data confidentiality, integrity, authenticity, and requires having a comprehensive key management plan that addresses the entire key lifecycle. The failure to adequately secure and manage this process can lead to data breaches, data loss, and legal and regulatory compliance challenges.

5.16   What are some common issues in ensuring the security of serverless architectures, and how can they be addressed?

Serverless architectures offer a lot of benefits over traditional architectures, such as improved scalability, better cost-effectiveness and faster development cycles. However, they also pose unique security challenges that organizations must be aware of and address to ensure that their applications and data are protected against cyber threats. Some of the most common issues faced in securing serverless architectures, along with their potential solutions, are mentioned below:

1. Inadequate Access Controls: One of the most significant security issues in serverless architectures is the lack of proper

access controls. A poorly configured access control system can give unauthorized users access to sensitive data, resulting in data breaches or loss of infrastructure. This can occur due to misconfigured IAM policies, unsecured API endpoints, or a poor choice of authentication mechanisms. To mitigate this risk, organizations need to adopt a least privilege approach and define strict policies for user access. They should also use multi-factor authentication and enforce secure password policies to minimize the risk of unauthorized access.

2. Lack of Visibility and Control: Another challenge with serverless architectures is the reduced visibility and control over the infrastructure. Since serverless platforms are managed by third-party providers, it can be challenging to monitor and detect security threats. This can result in critical security issues going unnoticed until it's too late. To address this challenge, organizations should regularly monitor their serverless architecture and leverage endpoint protection tools like antivirus and intrusion detection software. They should also use log analysis tools to monitor the activity on the serverless platform and identify any malicious activity.

3. Network Security: Serverless architectures rely heavily on APIs and microservices to handle critical business processes, which means that network security is crucial. An insecure API can lead to data breaches and other security threats. To address this challenge, organizations should use SSL/TLS encryption to secure all communication channels between services. They should also implement secure coding practices to prevent common API vulnerabilities such as SQL injection and cross-site scripting.

4. Resource Exhaustion: A poorly designed and maintained serverless architecture can be vulnerable to resource exhaustion

attacks, such as denial-of-service (DoS) attacks. Hackers can overload the application with excessive resource usage, which can disrupt the system's operations or even crash the serverless platform. To mitigate this risk, organizations should implement measures to limit resource usage, like rate-limiting and traffic throttling. This can help prevent resource exhaustion attacks and ensure the smooth functioning of the entire system.

Overall, securing a serverless architecture requires a combination of best practices and security-centric design. Organizations must also stay abreast of the latest security threats and emerging attack techniques to keep up with the evolving threat landscape. Relying on security experts and cybersecurity tools can also be helpful in identifying and mitigating security risks.

5.17   How do you approach developing and maintaining an effective vulnerability management program?

Developing and maintaining an effective vulnerability management program involves a comprehensive approach that includes continuous monitoring, risk assessment, prioritization, remediation, and reporting. The program should be designed to identify, manage and remediate vulnerabilities in a systematic and consistent manner. Here are some steps that can help:

1. Identify your assets: The first step of a vulnerability management program is to identify all your assets, including hardware, software, and data. This will help you prioritize the vulnerabilities that you need to address.

2. Conduct regular vulnerability scans: Conducting regular vulnerability scans using automated tools and manual methods can help you identify potential security loopholes in your IT infrastructure. These scans must be scheduled frequently enough to keep up with changing threats and software versions.

3. Prioritize vulnerabilities: Once vulnerabilities have been identified, it's important to evaluate them based on their potential impact on your network and prioritize them accordingly. This often uses a scoring system to determine severity and likelihood of successful exploitation.

4. Remediate vulnerabilities: This is the process of fixing vulnerabilities that have been identified as part of the vulnerability management program. This should be done immediately for high severity vulnerabilities to mitigate risk.

5. Monitor and verify remediation: Once vulnerabilities have been fixed, it's important to verify that the remediation was successful and no new vulnerabilities are introduced.

6. Continuous improvement: A vulnerability management program should be constantly reviewed and refined to adapt to the changing IT landscape and threat landscape. This includes periodic reviews of the scoring system, process, and reports.

7. Communication and reporting: Senior management should be regularly informed about the status of the vulnerability management program. Also, if a vulnerability has an impact on customers or partners, it should be reported to them too.

An example of a vulnerability management program in action is a organization that conducts regular vulnerability scans and patch management for its software and hardware systems. For example, if a vulnerability is discovered in a widely used software product, such as Adobe Reader, the organization would immediately update the software to fix the vulnerability. They would also create a patch management process that automates updates to software vulnerabilities, which ensures the timely installation of patches. By doing this, they can ensure that their network is secure and that they are always up-to-date with the latest security patches.

5.18   What are some best practices for securing the software supply chain and preventing supply chain attacks?

Securing the software supply chain is a critical aspect of preventing supply chain attacks. Here are some best practices that can help in securing the software supply chain:

1. Risk Assessment: Risk assessment should be carried out on all third-party software in use, especially those that have access to sensitive data. This risk assessment could be based on several factors such as the reputation of the vendor, quality of the software, and the level of access it has.

2. Code Review: Reviewing the code of third-party software components helps to detect any vulnerabilities or malicious code. This review should be performed regularly and should involve a team of experienced software developers.

3. Secure Architecture: The software supply chain should be designed to ensure that all components have an adequate level of security. This includes building secure architecture, secure

coding practices, and proper authentication mechanisms.

4. Verification and Validation: Verification and validation should be carried out at every stage of development to ensure that the software components are free from vulnerabilities and comply with security standards.

5. Regular Updates and Patches: Software updates and patches should be applied regularly to ensure that there are no vulnerabilities and to fix any existing vulnerabilities.

6. Vendor Management: Vendor management is an essential aspect of securing the software supply chain. The vendor should be selected based on their reputation, commitment to security standards, and transparency of their development process.

7. Employee Training: Employee training is critical in preventing supply chain attacks. Employees should be educated on the importance of security, secure coding practices, and the potential risks of using third-party software.

8. Incident Response Plan: An incident response plan should be in place to ensure that appropriate action is taken promptly in the event of a supply chain attack.

In summary, securing the software supply chain is an ongoing process that requires attention and diligence. A comprehensive security plan that involves regular risk assessments, code reviews, secure architecture design, and vendor management can help prevent supply chain attacks.

5.19 Can you discuss the role of privacy engineering in the development of secure systems?

Privacy engineering is the process of designing and building privacy-preserving systems by implementing security measures that protect the privacy of individuals' personal data throughout the entire lifecycle of the system.

The role of privacy engineering in the development of secure systems is multifaceted. By ensuring privacy engineering is implemented in the development of secure systems, three benefits can be achieved:

1. Protection of personal data:

Privacy engineering ensures personal data is protected against unauthorized access, use, disclosure, alteration, or destruction. By implementing privacy engineering measures, developers can ensure that the personal data collected is only used for its intended purpose and is protected against malicious attacks.

For example, encryption is a common privacy engineering technique that is used to protect personal data. Encryption ensures the data is transformed into an unreadable format, which cannot be accessed by unauthorized users even if they gain access to the system.

2. Compliance with regulations:

Privacy engineering is essential for ensuring compliance with various regulations and standards that govern data privacy. Regulations such as GDPR (General Data Protection Regula-

tion) and CCPA (California Consumer Privacy Act) have strict
data privacy requirements.

By implementing privacy engineering strategies, development
teams can ensure that the system complies with the relevant
regulations and data privacy standards.

3. User trust and confidence:

Users want to know that their personal data is being protected
and handled in a responsible manner. By implementing privacy engineering measures, developers can build a system that
protects the user's personal data privacy.

For example, Facebook announced the implementation of privacy engineering in its platform. The company implemented
a feature called Off-Facebook Activity which allows users the
ability to see a summary of the apps and websites that have
shared their data with Facebook, and to clear this information
from their account if needed.

This move has enhanced user trust with the platform, as individuals are now better informed of how their personal information is being utilized.

In conclusion, privacy engineering is crucial in ensuring that
secure systems are developed with a user's privacy in mind,
which can ultimately lead to increased user trust and confidence
in the system. In addition, it also helps the system remain
compliant with regulations and ensures that personal data is
protected throughout the entire system's life cycle.

5.20   What are some emerging trends and challenges in cybersecurity that organizations should be aware of?

Organizations today are facing a continually evolving set of cybersecurity threats and challenges that require constant vigilance and adaptation to stay protected. Here are some emerging trends and challenges that organizations should be aware of:

1. Cloud Security: One of the most significant trends in cybersecurity is the migration of data and applications to the cloud. With cloud-based services and storage becoming more ubiquitous, organizations face new challenges in ensuring the security of their data and systems.

2. Cyber Crime: Cyber criminals are becoming more sophisticated and persistent in their attacks, and are constantly evolving their tactics to stay ahead of security measures. One of the biggest challenges for organizations today is staying ahead of the latest threats and implementing effective cybersecurity measures to keep their systems and data safe.

3. IoT Security: As more devices become connected to the internet, the risk of cyber attacks targeting these devices is also increasing. Organizations need to consider the security implications of connected devices and implement appropriate security measures to prevent these devices from becoming a weak point in their security defenses.

4. Artificial Intelligence and Machine Learning: As AI and machine learning become more prevalent in cybersecurity, organizations are exploring new ways to leverage these technologies

to improve their security defenses. However, AI and machine learning can also be used by cyber criminals to develop more sophisticated attacks, which creates new challenges for organizations to stay protected.

5. Insider Threats: Insider threats, whether intentional or unintentional, continue to be a significant source of cybersecurity risk for organizations. Organizations need to implement effective monitoring and controls to detect and prevent insider threats, and educate employees on cybersecurity best practices.

6. Regulations and Standards: In addition to the evolving threat landscape, organizations also need to be aware of the changing regulatory environment for cybersecurity. Compliance requirements and standards such as GDPR and PCI DSS can place additional demands on organizations to maintain effective cybersecurity measures, and non-compliance can result in significant penalties and reputational damage.

In summary, organizations need to be aware of these emerging trends and challenges in cybersecurity and take appropriate measures to protect their data and systems. This requires a proactive and holistic approach to cybersecurity, including ongoing risk assessments, training and education, and a commitment to continuous improvement in cybersecurity practices.

Chapter 6

Guru

6.1 Can you discuss the implications of quantum computing on cryptography and cybersecurity, and how organizations can prepare for these changes?

Quantum computing is a newer form of computing that builds on the principles of quantum mechanics, which allows for the creation of quantum bits (qubits) that can exist in two states at once. Unlike traditional bits which can only exist in a state of either 0 or 1, qubits can exist in both 0 and 1 simultaneously. Because of this, quantum computing has the potential to revolutionize the computing industry by drastically increasing the speed and power of computing operations.

However, with the rise of quantum computing also come significant implications for cryptography and cybersecurity. Todays encryption algorithms, which are used to protect sensitive data in transit and at rest, rely on the difficulty of factorization and prime number multiplication to prevent unauthorized access. These algorithms are designed to be very difficult to solve using traditional computers, requiring an enormous amount of computational power and time.

Quantum computers, on the other hand, could potentially solve these algorithms in a matter of seconds, which would make it much easier for malicious actors to break into secure systems and steal sensitive information. This means that current encryption protocols may no longer be sufficient, and new quantum-resistant encryption methods will need to be developed.

Some ways organizations can prepare for the changes brought about by quantum computing are:

1. Invest in quantum-resistant encryption protocols: Security researchers are already working on developing new encryption that is resistant to quantum attacks. Organizations should be prepared to invest in the development and implementation of these quantum-resistant encryption methods as they become available.

2. Monitor developments in quantum computing: Organizations should keep a close eye on the development and deployment of quantum computing technology to understand the risks and prepare accordingly.

3. Plan for a post-quantum world: As quantum computing technology continues to progress, it may be necessary to plan for a post-quantum world where traditional encryption is no longer effective. Organizations should be prepared to move to

newer, more secure encryption methods as necessary.

4. Encrypt data at rest and in transit: Even though traditional encryption methods may be rendered ineffective by quantum computing, it is still important to encrypt data at rest and in transit. This buys time for organizations to implement post-quantum encryption methods and maintain security.

In conclusion, the development of quantum computing has significant implications for cryptography and cybersecurity. Organizations must be prepared to invest in new encryption protocols and closely monitor developments in quantum computing to maintain security in a post-quantum world.

6.2   What are some advanced techniques for automating the process of threat hunting and incident response?

Advanced techniques for automating the process of threat hunting and incident response include:

1. Machine learning and AI: These technologies can be used to detect anomalies, identify patterns and predict possible attacks. For example, machine learning algorithms can be trained to identify patterns in network traffic that indicate suspicious activity, such as command-and-control (C2) communications between an infected host and a remote attacker. Once the algorithm has learned these patterns, it can alert the security team of any future suspicious network activity.

2. Threat intelligence feeds: Automated tools can ingest threat

intelligence feeds from reputable sources and use that information to identify potential threats. For example, tools like Splunk or ELK can be configured to automatically search and parse external threat intelligence feeds for indicators of compromise (IOCs) that match the organization's network.

3. Playbooks: Playbooks are pre-set workflows that can be triggered automatically in response to specific events, such as a security incident. For example, a playbook could be configured to isolate a machine when it detects suspicious activity. Once triggered, the playbook can automatically execute the necessary steps to isolate the machine, such as shutting off network connectivity or taking a snapshot of the system for forensic analysis.

4. Automation scripts: These are custom-written utilities that automate repetitive tasks, such as collecting and analyzing logs, creating firewall rules, and searching for IOCs. For example, a script could be created to automatically block traffic from a specific IP address based on a set of predefined rules.

5. Security orchestration, automation and response (SOAR) platforms: These platforms automate the entire incident response process and integrate multiple security tools into a single workflow. For example, a SOAR platform could be configured to automatically launch a playbook in response to a specific event, such as a malware detection. Once triggered, the playbook can automatically collect and analyze logs, search for IOCs, isolate the affected machine, and alert the security team.

In conclusion, by leveraging these advanced techniques, organizations can significantly streamline their threat hunting and incident response efforts, leading to faster and more efficient incident detection and response, ultimately leading to better protection against cyber attacks.

6.3 How do you approach designing a security program to address the unique challenges of critical infrastructure protection?

Designing a security program for critical infrastructure protection requires a thoughtful and comprehensive approach. Below are steps that should be taken to ensure a strong security program.

1. Identify and assess potential risks: Before designing a security program, it is important to identify threats and potential risks that are unique to critical infrastructure. This involves understanding vulnerabilities and conducting risk assessments to help identify potential impacts resulting from an attack or breach.

2. Establish security objectives: From the risks identified, the organization should establish security objectives that reflect the desired state of the security environment. Objectives should be specific and measureable to allow security to be tracked and evaluated over time.

3. Develop a security plan: The security plan should be tailored to address the specific risks identified, security objectives, and organizational needs. This plan should include physical security measures, information security measures, and cybersecurity measures.

4. Implement and test the security program: Once the security plan has been developed, it is essential to put it into action. This often involves implementing new hardware and software technologies, as well as training personnel on new security protocols. It is important to conduct regular testing to ensure that the security program is effective and up-to-date.

5. Continuously evaluate and improve the security program: As the threat landscape continues to evolve, it is critical to continually evaluate the security program to ensure that it remains effective. Organizations can track the success of the security program by measuring progress towards security objectives, conducting regular vulnerability assessments and penetration testing, and ensuring that personnel remain up-to-date with ongoing training.

Examples of specific security measures that could be implemented as part of a comprehensive critical infrastructure protection program include:

- - Multi-factor authentication for access control to physical and digital systems

- - Network segmentation to isolate critical systems from non-critical systems and prevent lateral movement of attackers

- - Intrusion detection and prevention systems to detect and respond to potential attacks

- - Regular security training and awareness campaigns for personnel to promote a security-conscious culture

- - Cybersecurity incident response planning to enable a

timely and effective response to security breaches, including regular testing of incident response plans.

In summary, designing a security program for critical infrastructure protection involves identifying and assessing potential risks, establishing security objectives, developing a security plan, implementing and testing the security program, and continuously evaluating and improving the program. It is an ongoing process that requires a proactive and adaptive approach to ensure that the security program remains effective in the face of evolving threats.

6.4 Can you discuss the concept of security by design and its importance in the development of new technologies and systems?

Security by design, also known as secure-by-design, is an approach to software and systems development that incorporates security measures from the very beginning of the planning and design stages. It means building in security features and protocols at every stage of development, rather than bolting them on as an afterthought. This approach is becoming increasingly important as technology becomes more pervasive in our daily lives, as it helps prevent vulnerabilities and cyber attacks.

The concept of security by design is critical because the security of a system cannot be guaranteed if security features are added at the end of the development process. By incorporating security into the design process, developers can identify potential

security risks early on and address them before they become
exploited by attackers. Security requirements should be considered as integral parts of the system design and should be
reviewed throughout the development and testing process.

Consider an example of a company that is developing a new
mobile application. If the development team does not include
security considerations from the beginning, the application may
be vulnerable to cyber attacks. For instance, if the application
stores user data, a hacker may be able to exploit the application
and gain unauthorized access to the confidential information.

Another example is in the design of an industrial control system.
If the system's design team does not consider security from the
get-go, attackers may be able to compromise the entire system
and inflict significant damage. This was the case in the well-
known Stuxnet attack, where attackers exploited a vulnerability
in a supervisory control and data acquisition (SCADA) system,
causing physical damage to an Iranian nuclear facility.

Security by design can also help reduce the cost and effort involved in addressing security issues later in the development
process. By identifying potential vulnerabilities early on, developers can better plan and allocate resources towards preventing vulnerabilities, rather than addressing them after the
system has been deployed.

In summary, security by design is a crucial approach that must
be adopted in the development of new technologies and systems. By incorporating security considerations from the onset,
developers can minimize the risk of vulnerabilities and cyber attacks, potentially reducing the significant costs associated with
security breaches.

6.5   What are some of the ethical considerations in cybersecurity, particularly in the context of offensive security operations?

Ethical considerations in cybersecurity are critical because any action taken in the context of cybersecurity operations can have serious consequences. This is especially true for offensive security operations, which include activities such as penetration testing, hacking, and other practices that are designed to test the security of an organization's information systems.

One of the most significant ethical considerations in offensive security operations is the potential for harm to the target organization. Offensive security operations can cause significant disruptions to an organization's operations, compromise confidential data, and damage its reputation. For this reason, it's essential to ensure that any offensive security operation is conducted with the explicit permission of the target organization, or within the bounds of the law if conducted by a law enforcement agency.

Another ethical consideration is the potential for unintended consequences. Offensive security operations can sometimes lead to unintended damage, such as causing system failures or introducing malware into a network. Therefore, these operations must be carefully planned, and the possible impact of any activity must be thoroughly evaluated before it is carried out.

A further ethical consideration is the potential impact of offensive security operations on individuals. These individuals might be employees of the target organization, who could potentially lose their jobs as a result of the disruption caused by an offensive security operation. Alternatively, the operation might inadvertently compromise personal data or violate the privacy of individuals who have no connection to the target organization. As such, it's crucial to ensure that any offensive security operation is conducted with the utmost care and respect for the rights of individuals.

One more crucial ethical consideration is the handling of vulnerabilities discovered during an offensive security operation. These vulnerabilities must be responsibly disclosed to the target organization to enable them to fix the issue, and to protect the organization from further damage. If vulnerabilities are not reported, or are used in a malicious manner, then the result could be significant harm both to the target organization and the general public.

In conclusion, offensive security operations must be planned, evaluated, and executed ethically to ensure that they are conducted transparently, legally, and responsibly. By following these ethical considerations, organizations can ensure that their cybersecurity efforts do not harm other organizations or individuals while still achieving their goals.

6.6   How do you approach managing the complex interdependencies between various cybersecurity frameworks, standards, and regulations?

Managing the complex interdependencies between various cybersecurity frameworks, standards, and regulations requires a systematic approach that takes into account the different requirements, objectives, and recommendations of each framework, standard, or regulation. The following steps can help in approaching this challenge:

1. Conduct a comprehensive inventory: Start by identifying all the cybersecurity frameworks, standards, and regulations that are relevant to your organization. This will help you understand the scope and complexity of the task ahead.

2. Analyze the requirements: Once you have identified the different frameworks, standards, and regulations, analyze their requirements and objectives. This will help you understand the commonalities and differences between them.

3. Identify the gaps: Identify any gaps or overlaps between the different frameworks, standards, and regulations. This will help you determine where additional controls are needed or where controls can be consolidated.

4. Develop an integrated approach: Develop an integrated cybersecurity approach that incorporates the requirements, objectives, and recommendations of the different frameworks, standards, and regulations. This approach should take into account the specific needs and risks of your organization.

5. Establish a governance structure: Establish a governance structure that ensures that the integrated approach is implemented consistently across the organization. This includes assigning responsibilities for implementing and monitoring the different frameworks, standards, and regulations.

6. Monitor and update: Monitor and update the integrated approach regularly to ensure that it remains relevant and ef-

fective. This includes reviewing changes to the different frameworks, standards, and regulations and incorporating them into the integrated approach.

For example, an organization may need to comply with the General Data Protection Regulation (GDPR), the Payment Card Industry Data Security Standard (PCI DSS), and the National Institute of Standards and Technology (NIST) Cybersecurity Framework. To manage the interdependencies between these frameworks, the organization would need to analyze the requirements of each framework, identify any gaps or overlaps, and develop an integrated approach that addresses all the requirements. This could involve implementing common controls such as access control, encryption, and monitoring, as well as specific controls to address the unique requirements of each framework. The organization would also need to establish a governance structure that ensures the integrated approach is implemented consistently across the organization and monitor and update the approach regularly to ensure it remains effective.

6.7   What are some advanced techniques for attributing cyberattacks to specific threat actors and understanding their motivations?

Attributing cyberattacks to specific threat actors can be a difficult task, but there are some advanced techniques that can be used to increase the chances of success. Some of these techniques include:

1. TTP Analysis: One technique that can be used to attribute cyberattacks is TTP (Tactics, Techniques, and Procedures) analysis. This involves analyzing the methods and tools
used by the attackers to carry out the attack. By understanding their TTP, experts can link attacks to specific threat actors
and groups.

For example, if a threat actor is known to use a specific type of
malware or exploit, and that same malware or exploit is used
in a recent cyber attack, it could be a strong indicator that the
same group is responsible for both attacks.

2. Malware Analysis: Another technique that can be used to
attribute cyberattacks is malware analysis. By analyzing the
code and behavior of the malware used in an attack, experts can
identify similarities with other malware used by known threat
actors. This can help to identify the group responsible for the
attack.

3. Network Forensics: Network forensics involves analyzing network traffic and logs to identify indicators of compromise. This
can include identifying patterns of activity that are consistent
with specific threat actors, such as IP addresses and domain
names used in previous attacks.

For example, if a threat actor is known to use a particular domain name in their attacks, and that domain name is identified
in network logs from a recent attack, it could be a strong indi-
cation that the same group is responsible.

4. Open Source Intelligence: Open source intelligence (OSINT)
involves gathering information from publicly available sources
to identify potential threat actors. This can include monitoring forums and social media platforms where cyber criminals

may discuss their activities, as well as tracking online payment systems and other financial transactions.

For example, if a group is known to accept payment through a specific online payment system, monitoring that payment system may reveal information about the group's activities and potential motivations.

5. Human Intelligence: Human intelligence involves gathering information from human sources, such as insiders or informants, to identify potential threat actors. This can be particularly useful in cases where the threat actor is a nation-state or large criminal organization.

For example, if an insider provides information about a group's activities and motivations, this can help to attribute cyberattacks to that group.

In conclusion, attributing cyberattacks to specific threat actors and understanding their motivations requires a combination of technical and non-technical techniques. By using these techniques in combination, experts can increase the chances of successful attribution and identify potential threat actors.

6.8   Can you discuss the role of game theory in modeling and understanding the behavior of adversaries in cyberspace?

Game theory is a mathematical tool used to study human behavior in strategic situations where the outcomes depend on the interactions among players. In the context of cybersecurity, game theory allows us to model the behavior of adversaries and understand their decision-making process based on their objectives and strategies.

One of the key applications of game theory in cybersecurity is the analysis of attacker-defender games, which involve two or more players, each with their own objectives and strategies. For example, consider a situation where a company wants to protect its computer network from a cyber attack, and an attacker wants to breach the network for their own purposes. The company can use game theory to model different attack scenarios and determine the best defense strategy, while the attacker can use game theory to model the company's defense mechanisms and develop a successful attack strategy.

Game theory can also be used to analyze the behavior of multiple attackers who may be acting in collaboration, competition, or independently. In this scenario, each attacker must decide whether to cooperate with other attackers, compete with them, or work independently. Game theory can help to determine the optimal strategies for each attacker as well as the overall equilibrium of the game.

Another application of game theory in cybersecurity is the study of strategic decision-making in the context of policy formulation. For example, consider the development of national cybersecurity policies. Game theory can help to model the incentives and objectives of different stakeholders, such as governments, industries, and individuals, and evaluate the impact of policy decisions on the overall security of cyberspace.

Finally, game theory can be used to analyze the impact of cyber attacks on the behavior of market players. For example, a successful cyber attack on a company may affect the prices of its stocks, which may in turn affect the behavior of other market players. Game theory can help to model the interactions between different market players and assess the impact of cyber attacks on the overall stability of the market.

Overall, game theory is a valuable tool for modeling and understanding the behavior of adversaries in cyberspace. By using game theory to analyze different scenarios, stakeholders can make more informed decisions about cyber defense, policy formulation, and market stability.

6.9 How do you approach the process of identifying and prioritizing security investments to optimize the allocation of resources and reduce risk?

To approach the process of identifying and prioritizing security investments, it is important to have a clear understanding of the organization's business objectives, its risk appetite, its regulatory requirements, its assets and their criticality, and its existing security posture. Here are some steps organizations can take to optimize the allocation of resources and reduce risk:

1. Conduct a risk assessment: A risk assessment is a systematic process of identifying, evaluating, and prioritizing risks to the organization's information assets. It is important to conduct a risk assessment to identify and prioritize security vulnerabilities and threats that pose the most significant risk to the organization.

2. Develop a risk management plan: Based on the outcomes

of the risk assessment, develop a risk management plan that outlines specific actions to minimize or mitigate the risks. The plan should identify key security controls that are required to protect the organization's assets and data.

3. Establish a security budget: Once the risk assessment and management plan are in place, establish a security budget that allocates resources appropriately to the highest-priority areas. The budget should focus on investing in measures that provide the greatest return on investment in terms of reducing risk.

4. Prioritize security investments: Prioritize the security investments based on the risk management plan. The highest-priority investments should be those that address the most significant risks to the organization. It is important to ensure that investments are aligned with the organization's business objectives and risk appetite.

5. Continuous monitoring and improvement: Security is an ongoing process that requires continuous monitoring and improvement. Regular security assessments should be conducted to identify new risks and vulnerabilities that may impact the organization's security posture. This can be done through regular penetration testing, vulnerability scanning, and security training for employees.

For example, if an organization identifies its critical assets as its customer data and its e-commerce platform, it may prioritize investments in encryption technologies, network security, and access controls. Similarly, if an organization operates in a highly regulated industry, it may prioritize investments in compliance and regulatory requirements. Ultimately, the approach to identifying and prioritizing security investments should be tailored to the specific needs and goals of the organization.

6.10   What are some novel approaches to detecting and mitigating insider threats within an organization?

Insider threats are often considered one of the most difficult cybersecurity challenges to address because insiders typically have authorized access to an organization's systems, data, and other critical resources. However, several novel approaches have emerged to address insider threats, including:

1. User behavior analytics (UBA): UBA is a type of cybersecurity solution that uses machine learning and big data analytics to detect anomalies in user behavior that may indicate an insider threat. UBA tools analyze user activity logs, network traffic, and other data sources to identify potential threats, such as unauthorized access attempts or data exfiltration.

2. Zero Trust security model: The Zero Trust security model is a holistic approach to cybersecurity that assumes no user or device can be trusted and requires strict authentication and access control policies for all access attempts. With the Zero Trust approach, each user must authenticate themselves at every step, and access permissions are granted based on a variety of factors, including location, device, and behavior.

3. Multifactor authentication (MFA): MFA is a security technique that requires users to provide multiple forms of identification, such as a password and a fingerprint scan, to access a system or data. Multifactor authentication is an effective way to prevent unauthorized access, even when an insider has valid credentials.

4. Continuous monitoring: Continuous monitoring involves

tracking users' activities in real-time or near real-time to detect any suspicious behavior or activities that may be indicative of an insider threat. This approach helps organizations identify and mitigate threats before they cause any significant damage or data loss.

5. Threat hunting: Threat hunting is a proactive approach to cybersecurity that involves actively searching for potential insider threats before they can cause any harm. Threat hunters use various techniques and tools, including network analysis, to identify unusual or suspicious patterns of behavior, such as repeated login attempts outside normal business hours.

6. Insider threat training programs: Insider threat training programs can help employees understand the risks of insider threats and how to recognize and report suspicious activities. Such training programs can be instrumental in establishing a culture of security and reducing the risks of insider threats.

These are some of the novel approaches taken to detect and mitigate insider threats within an organization. However, it is essential to note that no single technique can be entirely effective in detecting and mitigating insider threats, and there needs to be a comprehensive approach to addressing the issue.

6.11   Can you discuss the challenges of securing emerging technologies, such as 5G, AI, and blockchain, and how organizations can prepare for these challenges?

Securing emerging technologies presents certain challenges that differ from traditional security threats. The characteristics and complexities of these technologies make them attractive targets for cybercriminals. Below are some of the significant challenges and recommendations to overcome them:

1. 5G Networks: The introduction of 5G networks represents significant security risks. The technology relies on virtualization, software-defined networking, and network slicing, which introduces multiple points of entry for cybercriminals. Moreover, 5G networks make use of internet of things (IoT) devices to communicate and exchange data, which increases the likelihood of cyber threats.

To secure 5G networks, organizations can do the following:

- - Implement end-to-end encryption to protect data as it flows from device to device.

- - Perform regular vulnerability scanning and penetration testing to detect and address weaknesses in the network.

- - Use access controls to prevent unauthorized access and restrict network access based on need-to-know principles.

- - Follow best practices for securing IoT devices, such as segmenting networks, disabling unnecessary services, and updating firmware regularly.

2. AI: AI systems can help organizations improve their operational efficiency and decision-making. However, AI also represents unique security challenges. Malicious actors can exploit vulnerabilities in the algorithms used by AI systems to carry out attacks, such as adversarial attacks or data poisoning attacks.

To secure AI systems, organizations can do the following:

- - Use only trusted and validated data to train AI models.

- - Regularly test AI models for vulnerabilities and perform code reviews.

- - Implement access controls to prevent unauthorized access to AI systems.

- - Follow best practices for securing cloud-based AI systems, such as encrypting data both in transit and at rest.

3. Blockchain: Blockchain technology can help organizations manage and secure their data. However, securing the blockchain network can be challenging, especially when it comes to providing end-to-end security for the data stored on the network.

To secure a blockchain network, organizations can do the following:

- - Implement end-to-end encryption for all data stored on the blockchain network.

- - Use access controls to restrict access to the blockchain network based on need-to-know principles.

- - Regularly test the network for vulnerabilities and perform code reviews.

- - Use smart contracts and digital signatures to ensure the authenticity and integrity of all transactions on the network.

In conclusion, securing emerging technologies require a strategic and proactive approach. Organizations must invest in the right resources and tools to prevent cyber threats effectively. Additionally, training staff members on emerging technologies and keeping up-to-date with the latest threats can also help to mitigate risks. By implementing best practices for securing these technologies, organizations can gain the benefits while reducing the associated risks.

6.12   How do you approach creating a comprehensive cyber risk management program that considers both technical and non-technical factors?

Creating a comprehensive cyber risk management program involves identifying, assessing, and mitigating potential risks to the organization's sensitive data, critical systems, and business operations. A successful cyber risk management program should consider both technical and non-technical factors to create a holistic and effective strategy. Here are some key steps that an organization can follow to create such a program:

1. Identify and classify assets: The first step in creating a comprehensive cyber risk management program is to identify and

classify all assets that are critical to the organization. This includes both physical and digital assets, such as servers, databases,
laptops, and mobile devices, as well as sensitive data and intellectual property.

2. Conduct a risk assessment: Once assets have been identified, its important to conduct a risk assessment to understand the potential impact and likelihood of a cyber-attack on
these assets. Technical factors such as vulnerabilities, software
and hardware weaknesses, and access controls should be taken
into consideration during this stage. Non-technical factors such
as employee training, company culture, and third-party risks
should also be taken into account.

3. Develop a risk management plan: Based on the risk assessment, a risk management plan should be developed that prior-
itizes the risks based on their potential impact and likelihood
of occurrence. The plan should identify mitigation strategies,
such as software patches, regular backups, access controls, and
employee training, that can be implemented to reduce the identified risks.

4. Implement security controls: Implementing technical security controls such as firewalls, intrusion detection and prevention systems, antivirus software, and encryption can help to
reduce the risk of cyber-attacks. Non-technical controls such as
policies, procedures, and employee training can also be implemented to strengthen the overall security posture of the organization.

5. Continuously monitor and evaluate the program: A comprehensive cyber risk management program should be constantly
monitored and evaluated to ensure that the controls are effective and relevant. If any new risks or potential threats are

identified, the program should be updated accordingly.

For example, an organization could have a security program that includes both technical and non-technical components. Technical solutions would include hardware firewall configuration, periodic penetration testing, advanced antivirus software deployment, and vulnerability scans. Non-technical solutions would include establishing security awareness training, implementing strict access policies, and maintaining strict device and application management processes.

In conclusion, creating a comprehensive cyber risk management program that considers both technical and non-technical factors requires a holistic approach that recognizes the dynamic nature of cybersecurity threats. It involves identifying assets and risks, implementing security controls, and continuously monitoring and evaluating the program. Ultimately, a successful cyber risk management program depends on the organization's commitment to security and a culture of cyber resilience.

6.13 What are some key considerations in developing and implementing a global cybersecurity strategy in a multinational organization?

Developing and implementing a global cybersecurity strategy in a multinational organization involves several key considerations, including:

1. Understanding the regulatory landscape: The regulatory landscape for cybersecurity can vary greatly between countries

and regions, and it's critical to understand the laws, regulations, and standards that apply to your organization's operations. For example, the European Union's General Data Protection Regulation (GDPR) imposes significant penalties on companies that fail to protect personal data, while China's Cybersecurity Law requires data localization and limits the transfer of certain data overseas.

2. Customizing security controls for different regions: Different regions may have unique threats and risk profiles, and it's important to tailor security controls to address these. For example, a multinational organization operating in the Middle East may need to have strong protections against cyberattacks from state-sponsored actors, while an organization operating in Southeast Asia may need to focus on mitigating the risks of ransomware attacks.

3. Establishing a strong governance framework: A comprehensive global cybersecurity strategy requires robust governance structures and accountability mechanisms that ensure all stakeholders understand their roles and responsibilities. This includes creating a clear organizational structure, defining clear policies and procedures, and establishing effective oversight mechanisms.

4. Aligning business goals with cybersecurity objectives: Cybersecurity must be integrated into the organization's overall business strategy, reflecting the specific needs and objectives of different business units. For example, an organization operating in the financial services sector may need to prioritize the security of customer data and financial transactions.

5. Ensuring effective communication and collaboration: Effective communication and collaboration are essential for the

success of a global cybersecurity strategy. This includes promoting cybersecurity awareness among employees, facilitating collaboration between different regional and functional teams, and building strong relationships with external partners, such as regulatory authorities and cybersecurity vendors.

Overall, developing and implementing a global cybersecurity strategy requires a proactive, risk-based approach that engages all stakeholders and accounts for the unique challenges and opportunities posed by operating in a multinational environment.

6.14   How can organizations effectively collaborate and share information to improve collective defense against cyber threats?

Effective collaboration and information sharing are critical for building a strong collective defense against cyber threats. Here are some ways organizations can achieve this:

1. Establish a common language and framework: It is important to develop a common language and framework for discussing cyber threats and attacks. This can help organizations understand each other's perspectives, share information effectively and respond to threats in a coordinated manner. The National Institute of Standards and Technology (NIST) Cybersecurity Framework is an example of a widely accepted language and framework that organizations can use to communicate their cybersecurity posture.

2.   Create formal partnerships and alliances: Organizations

can form partnerships and alliances with other organizations to share threat intelligence, collaborate on cybersecurity research, and coordinate incident response. For example, the Cyber Threat Alliance is a formal partnership of cybersecurity companies that shares threat intelligence and research to improve collective defense against cyber threats.

3. Join ISACs: Information Sharing and Analysis Centers (ISACs) are organizations that facilitate information sharing among their members in a specific industry or sector. By joining an ISAC, organizations can gain access to timely and relevant threat intelligence and collaborate with other members to improve their cybersecurity posture.

4. Invest in technology and tools: Organizations can invest in technology and tools that facilitate information sharing and collaboration. For example, threat intelligence platforms enable organizations to collect, process and share threat intelligence with their partners and stakeholders in a timely and effective manner.

5. Develop clear policies and procedures: Organizations should develop clear policies and procedures for sharing information and collaborating with other organizations. These policies should specify what information can be shared, with whom, and how. They should also outline the roles and responsibilities of different stakeholders in the collaboration process to ensure that everyone is on the same page.

6. Foster a culture of collaboration: Finally, organizations should foster a culture of collaboration by encouraging communication, trust, and transparency. This can be achieved by organizing regular meetings, training sessions and workshops to facilitate knowledge sharing and communication among em-

ployees and stakeholders.

In summary, effective collaboration and information sharing are essential for improving collective defense against cyber threats. Organizations can achieve this by establishing a common language and framework, forming partnerships and alliances, joining ISACs, investing in technology and tools, developing clear policies and procedures, and fostering a culture of collaboration.

6.15   Can you discuss the concept of active cyber defense and its role in an organization's security posture?

Active cyber defense refers to a proactive approach to cybersecurity that involves actively monitoring an organization's network and systems, actively seeking out and identifying potential threats or attackers, and taking offensive measures to neutralize those threats.

The goal of active cyber defense is to prevent attacks by identifying and eliminating threats before they can cause damage. This approach is different from traditional cybersecurity methods, which are largely reactive and focus on detecting and responding to attacks after they have already occurred.

One example of active cyber defense is honeypots, which are decoy systems that are designed to look like real targets to attackers. When an attacker tries to access a honeypot, the system will trigger an alert and allow security professionals to identify and analyze the attacker's techniques and tactics.

Another example of active cyber defense is the use of threat intelligence feeds. These feeds provide organizations with real-time information about known threats and vulnerabilities, which can help them identify and prioritize security risks and take steps to proactively mitigate those risks.

Active cyber defense can play a critical role in an organization's security posture. By proactively identifying and neutralizing threats before they can cause damage, organizations can reduce the impact of cyber attacks and better protect their systems and data.

However, it's important to note that active cyber defense should be used in conjunction with other cybersecurity measures, such as strong access controls, employee training, and regular security assessments. Active cyber defense is not a silver bullet solution and should be viewed as just one component of a comprehensive cybersecurity strategy.

6.16 What are some key considerations in ensuring the security and privacy of biometric authentication systems?

Biometric authentication systems are being increasingly used as a more secure and convenient way of authentication than traditional methods, such as passwords or PINs. However, ensuring the security and privacy of biometric authentication systems requires careful consideration of several key factors to protect the sensitive personal information used for these systems. Here are some key considerations in ensuring the security and privacy of biometric authentication systems:

1. Data encryption: Data encryption is a crucial aspect for protecting sensitive biometric data from being accessed by unauthorized users or cybercriminals. Biometric data should always
be encrypted both when it is stored and transmitted across
networks.

2. Access control: Access control mechanisms should be implemented to ensure that only authorized personnel can access
biometric data. This includes strong user authentication procedures, such as multi-factor authentication, and limiting data
access to specific individuals based on their roles.

3. Identity authentication: It is essential to verify the identity
of the user before granting access to sensitive biometric data.
This can be achieved through various means such as fingerprint
scanning or facial recognition. However, it is important to use
secure and reliable biometric scanning devices to ensure that
an attacker cannot bypass the system and gain unauthorized
access.

4. System security: Biometric authentication systems should be
designed with security in mind. Particular attention should be
given to access control, network protocols, and the prevention
of unauthorized software modifications. Additionally, regular
security testing and vulnerability assessments should be conducted to identify and fix software and hardware vulnerabilities
that could be exploited by attackers.

5. Data retention and destruction: Biometric data retention
policies should be established, and once the data is no longer
needed, it should be securely destroyed. The process of destruction should leave no possibility of retrieval by unauthorized personnel.

6. Transparency and consent: Biometric authentication systems operate with sensitive personal information, so it is important to be transparent with users about how their data will be used and obtain informed consent before collecting or using their biometric data.

For example, facial recognition systems used in airports allow the passenger to scan their ID and glance at a camera for recognition. Still, it's important to consider how long the airport will store the data and who will have access to the data collected. Ensuring transparency and consent can help build user trust in biometric authentication systems, ultimately increasing their adoption and success.

Overall, implementing security and privacy practices that are appropriate for biometric authentication systems can protect users' sensitive personal information from malicious exploitation while also providing a more secure and convenient authentication process.

6.17   How do you approach the challenge of securing data in transit, at rest, and in use across a complex and diverse IT environment?

Securing data in transit, at rest, and in use is a challenge that requires a comprehensive and strategic approach. Here are some steps that can be taken to overcome this challenge:

1. Conduct a thorough risk assessment: Identify the types and volume of data in your environment, how they are stored, and

who has access to them. Also, identify the possible risk scenarios that can compromise data confidentiality, integrity, and
availability.

2. Establish a data protection policy: Create a policy that
outlines the types of data to be protected, the measures to be
taken to protect them, and the consequences of non-compliance.
The policy should also define the roles and responsibilities of
all parties involved in data protection.

3. Implement strong access controls: Grant access to data only
to those authorized to access them. Use strong authentication
and authorization mechanisms to control who can access data
and what actions they can perform.

4. Encrypt data in transit and at rest: Use encryption technologies to protect data in transit and at rest. This ensures
that even if data is intercepted or stolen, it will be unreadable
by unauthorized parties.

5. Regularly back up data: In the event of a data breach or
loss, having a backup ensures that data can be recovered and
restored. Regularly backing up data also helps to maintain data
integrity and availability.

6. Implement intrusion detection and prevention mechanisms:
Use IDS/IPS technologies to monitor network traffic and detect
and prevent unauthorized access or activity that can compromise data security.

7. Train your staff: Educate your staff on the importance of
data protection and the role they play in maintaining it. Provide them with regular training on best practices for data protection and ensure they understand the consequences of failing

to adhere to the policy.

For example, a healthcare organization may implement secure messaging systems to ensure that patient data is encrypted in transit, invest in a data backup solution to store all records, and use a network security solution to protect their systems from cyber attacks. All these measures would help secure data in transit, at rest, and in use in their complex and diverse IT environment.

6.18 What are some advanced techniques for conducting penetration testing and red team exercises to simulate real-world cyberattacks?

Penetration testing and red team exercises are critical components of a comprehensive cybersecurity program. These exercises help organizations identify vulnerabilities and evaluate the effectiveness of their defense mechanisms against cyberattacks. Here are some advanced techniques for conducting penetration testing and red team exercises to simulate real-world cyberattacks:

1. Social engineering: Social engineering is an advanced technique for penetrating an organization's network by exploiting human behavior. It involves tricking employees into divulging sensitive information or clicking on malicious links. Penetration testers and red teamers can use social engineering techniques, such as phishing emails, and phone-based attacks to gain access to an organization's network.

2. Zero-day exploits: Zero-day exploits are vulnerabilities in software or hardware that are unknown to the developers. Penetration testers and red teamers can use these exploits to test an organizations security and evaluate how quickly the organization can detect and respond to an attack.

3. Advanced persistent threat (APT) attacks: APT attacks are sophisticated attacks that are designed to gain access to an organization's network and remain undetected for an extended period. Penetration testers and red teamers can use APT attack techniques, such as using advanced malware that evades detection, to evaluate an organization's detection and response capabilities.

4. Wireless network testing: Wireless networks create an additional layer of vulnerability that cyber attackers can exploit easily. Advanced penetration testers and red teamers can use wireless network testing techniques, such as war-driving and spoofing, to identify weaknesses in wireless networks and gain unauthorized access to an organization's network.

5. Threat emulation: Threat emulation involves creating a realistic simulation of a specific threat actor or attack to test an organization's security. This technique allows penetration testers and red teamers to evaluate an organization's ability to detect and respond to specific cyberattacks.

6. Infiltration testing: Infiltration testing involves simulating a real-world cyberattack by attempting to gain unauthorized access to an organization's network by using advanced techniques. This technique involves a combination of social engineering, zero-day exploits, and APT techniques.

In summary, conducting penetration testing and red team exercises using advanced techniques is an essential aspect of a comprehensive cybersecurity program. These exercises simulate real-world cyberattacks and help organizations identify and remediate vulnerabilities before cyber criminals can exploit them for nefarious purposes.

6.19 How do you approach the process of ensuring that cybersecurity solutions are both technically effective and legally compliant?

Ensuring that cybersecurity solutions are both technically effective and legally compliant is a critical aspect of any cybersecurity strategy. Here are some steps you can take to ensure your cybersecurity measures meet these requirements:

1. Understand relevant regulations and compliance frameworks: It's essential to have a deep understanding of the specific regulations or compliance frameworks that impact your industry or organization. For example, if you are dealing with healthcare data, you need to be familiar with HIPAA regulations. You should also have a good understanding of other frameworks like PCI-DSS, GDPR, and CCPA, etc., and how they apply to your organization.

2. Identify technical solutions that align with regulations and compliance requirements: Once you have a good understanding of the regulations and frameworks that apply to your organization, it's important to identify technical solutions that align with these requirements. For example, if you need to comply with HIPAA, you may need to implement encryption,

two-factor authentication, and secure communications channels for sensitive patient data.

3. Evaluate the effectiveness of technical solutions: It's vital to evaluate the effectiveness of technical solutions to ensure they meet your security requirements. This can involve penetration testing, vulnerability assessments, and other security tests to ensure that your security measures are effective and able to deter or prevent cyber threats.

4. Align your security measures with your organizational objectives: Cybersecurity solutions need to be aligned with your organizational objectives, as well as legal requirements. For example, if you value speed of business processes, you may implement automation and cloud services. Also, you may choose to trade-off security for business requirements in certain situations like in Agile methodology.

5. Establish a robust compliance program: Cybersecurity compliance is an ongoing process that requires continuous monitoring and review to ensure that your organization remains in compliance with relevant regulations and frameworks. You should establish a robust compliance program that includes ongoing risk assessments, regular testing and auditing, and incident-response procedures to respond to any breaches of security that might occur.

By following these steps, you can ensure that your cybersecurity measures are both technically effective and legally compliant, which helps to reduce the risk of cyber-attacks and protect your organization's valuable assets.

6.20   Can you discuss the concept of cyber diplomacy and its role in promoting international cooperation on cybersecurity issues?

Cyber diplomacy refers to diplomatic efforts aimed at resolving cybersecurity issues and promoting international cooperation on such issues. Cybersecurity is a global problem that requires international cooperation and coordination. Cybercrime is not restricted by national borders and international cooperation is necessary to address global threats.

The role of cyber diplomacy is to create an environment of trust and cooperation among nations. It aims to foster cooperation and collaboration among nations, to develop common strategies and frameworks for cybersecurity, to build technical capabilities, and to promote exchanges of information and best practices. Cyber diplomacy can take place through bilateral talks, multilateral meetings, and international conferences.

One example of successful cyber diplomacy is the Budapest Convention on Cybercrime. The Budapest Convention was adopted by the Council of Europe in 2001 and is the first international treaty dealing with cybercrime. It provides a framework for international cooperation on cybersecurity issues such as cybercrime, data protection, and electronic evidence.

Another example of successful cyber diplomacy is the US-China Cyber Agreement. The agreement was reached in 2015, and it aimed to address concerns about state-sponsored cyberattacks targeting businesses, the theft of intellectual property, and other cyber threats. The agreement demonstrated the ability of nations to work together to mitigate cybersecurity risks in a rapidly evolving digital environment.

Overall, cyber diplomacy plays an essential role in promoting international cooperation on cybersecurity issues. It can help to establish common cybersecurity standards, build trust, and encourage nations to collaborate to develop technical capabilities for cybersecurity. By working together, nations can combat cyber threats more effectively while respecting each other's sovereignty and interests.